P9-BHU-375

Trina Marx has studied tap dance extensively
with several great tap artists and has taught
throughout the greater New York area
to people of all ages. She is working
toward her doctorate in the healing arts.

Trina Marx

TAP DANCE
A BEGINNER'S GUIDE

Photography by Therese Mazzetti

A SPECTRUM BOOK

Prentice-Hall, Inc., Englewood Cliffs, New Jersey 07632

Library of Congress Cataloging in Publication Data

Marx, Trina   (date).
   Tap dance.

   "A Spectrum Book."
   Includes index.
   1. Tap dancing.   2. Tap dancing—History.
I. Title.
GV1794.M27 1983   793.3'24   83-3294
ISBN 0-13-884650-2
ISBN 0-13-884643-X (pbk.)

© 1983 by Prentice-Hall, Inc., Englewood Cliffs, New Jersey 07632.
All rights reserved. No part of this book may be reproduced in any form
or by any means without permission in writing from the publisher.
A Spectrum Book. Printed in the United States of America.

This book is available at a special discount when ordered in
bulk quantities. Contact Prentice-Hall, Inc., General
Publishing Division, Special Sales, Englewood Cliffs, N.J. 07632.

10 9 8 7 6 5 4 3 2 1

ISBN 0-13-884650-2

ISBN 0-13-884643-X {PBK.}

Editorial/production supervision by Maxine Bartow and Rita Young
Cover design by Hal Siegel
Manufacturing buyers: Christine Johnston and Edward J. Ellis

All photographs (with the exception of the photographs on pp. 103, 152, and
159) and drawings (with the exception of the drawing on p. 162) are by
Therese Mazzetti.

The drawing on p. 162 is by Anna Marie Ottaviano.

The photograph on p. 152 is by Zachary Freyman from the Dance Collection.
Used by permission of The New York Public Library at Lincoln Center, Astor,
Lenox and Tilden Foundations and Zachary Freyman.

Prentice-Hall International, Inc., *London*
Prentice-Hall of Australia Pty. Limited, *Sydney*
Prentice-Hall Canada Inc., *Toronto*
Prentice-Hall of India Private Limited, *New Delhi*
Prentice-Hall of Japan, Inc., *Tokyo*
Prentice-Hall of Southeast Asia Pte. Ltd., *Singapore*
Whitehall Books Limited, *Wellington, New Zealand*
Editora Prentice-Hall do Brasil Ltda., *Rio de Janeiro*

Contents

Foreword

There is the music. For the tap dancer there is always the music; the tap-dancer is the music, the composer as well as the choreographer. Skill, musicality, discipline, and exuberance are the essentials; then come taste, conception, accuracy, and ultimately the performance.

Tap dance is a performance art, and how the dancer presents the material is as important in some instances as the material itself. Because personality is so connected with this form, it too must have a high level of artistry. Perhaps this is one of the reasons that tap dance is so often misunderstood and is not closely examined as an art form. Delivery can so beguile the audience that the execution of the steps and complexity of composition are not thoroughly examined. But for this art to continue and develop, the audience must develop with it, give up some of its affection for nostalgia, and begin to listen seriously to the themes and ideas the artist is developing.

In this time of the tap revival it is urgent that critics and students become discerning and pay attention to patterns, accents, punctuations, and body moves that have taken years to develop. They must perceive the uniqueness of each individual artist, for each tap-dancer struggles to find a unique statement. We cannot only ask who is the best dancer, but also what is each dancer saying and how well. In this form, the public insists on fingering the best and dismissing the rest. Tap dance is not a race to the finish line; it is an art form, with as many shapes, colors, and concepts as the world of modern dance and ballet with the added ingredient of musical composition. We must nurture the dancer and exponents of this form by trying to know and appreciate what the form encompasses. There is nothing so disheartening after pouring years of sweat into material than reading a critical analysis that states emphatically, "They were terrific and wore blue suits."

It is of utmost importance that teachers instruct students in the history of this form so that they might know the difference between traditional patterns and experimentation. If students are aware of the incredible range inherent in tap dance, their vision will not be trapped by a one-dimensional analysis or application. The resurgence of tap dance, this truly American art form, has been a long time coming. Now we must discover how we can encourage rather than restrict its growth.

This book allows the student and appreciator access into the back rooms of many fine and divergent dancers. I hope that it will shed light on a dance form that can live as long as the dancer lives and keep getting better.

Brenda Bufalino
tap artist

1

Introduction

Throughout its history, tap dancing has been portrayed as a happy, carefree form of movement. Movies and theater classically depict the smiling tap-dancer as "footloose and fancy-free," without a worry in the world, a free spirit having an enjoyable time, jovial to the point of lacking any seriousness. This sparkle is augmented by the fact that the dancers are often skilled in the art of tap and performing; they have an uncanny ability to manifest this skill with an air of buoyancy and delight, charming their audiences with flair and ease. They seem to share their movement and expression so that everyone feels embraced. What this marvelous rapport does not seem to convey, however, is the complexity involved in the mastering of the form.

The fundamental feature of tap dance is the use of both feet as a musical instrument. Two metal pieces are placed on the sole of the shoe: one covering the area from the ball of the foot to the tip of the toe, the other covering the entire heel area (this is not a set rule, as some dancers prefer a smaller toe tap). The object of this dance form is to master the use of the feet and body in playing melodic patterns and drumming out rhythms, the sounds of which are produced by the contact of the metal on the floor. Although the production of the sound is limited to the toes and heels, the variations in dynamics and actual rhythms are myriad. The sides of the tap, the tip of the toe, and the ball of the foot all yield different qualities of sound. The texture of the tap sound, or how hard or soft the foot makes contact with the floor, also allows for tremendous audible variation. What allows for the greatest versatility, though, is the syncopation or tempo at which the step is executed, as well as the exact placement of the particular step. This provides tap dance with a unique distinction—no matter how many times you perform a step, a time will come when that exact maneuver will seem new, because of the tempo or the style of the person showing the step.

To an innocent observer, tap appears to be concentrated in the feet because they are where the sounds emerge. Yet the ability to perform the actual movements is dependent on one's ability to incorporate body movement.

Rapid footwork has a tendency to distract one's attention from the body, but the step is virtually impossible without precise body placement, no matter how subtle. As in any form of movement, exact positioning is emphasized and more obvious when the step is performed slowly.

In learning any form of dance or sport, your purpose is to train the body to memorize the exact positions necessary to perform the movement. This kind of memory is achieved through repetition and constant guidance, to the point where little or no conscious thought is required for the movement to occur. Just as words flow in speech, movements emanate from the body of a well-trained dancer with fluidity and articulation. Similarly, when we learn to write, the hand is an unfamiliar tool that is difficult to control, consequently making formation of the symbols laborious. As hand usage increases, dexterity improves, and the ability to draw smaller, more elaborate symbols becomes easier. In tap dance, the same rules apply. One begins with exaggerated movements that teach the body and feet the correct placement. As the steps become more familiar, the capacity to condense the movement and go faster is acquired.

Experiment with body positioning. If a particular step seems very difficult, try keeping your feet closer together and more directly under the hips. Or try taking larger or smaller steps. In a classroom situation, pay close attention to the body placement of the instructor and then adapt the movement to your own body. It is also important to begin experiencing body weight changes. Placing all the body weight on one foot at a time, shift from side to side. Then make the movement smoother and lighter, until you feel comfortable.

A practical way to begin a tap warm-up is by simply walking forward, backward, and sideways at various tempos. Something as natural as walking at different paces and in different directions loosens and warms the body while it simultaneously improves concentration. Silly as it may seem, walking may suddenly become difficult; you may start swinging the right arm as you step with your right foot, contrary to the way you normally would. Usually when you step with your left leg, the right arm naturally swings forward (and remember that it is often said that if you can walk you can dance.) At this point it is advantageous for the beginner to focus on developing a keen ear and good concentration. Try to direct your energy and avoid thinking about other things that may be going on in your life, so you can incorporate the information and begin to dance. The next rudiments that will be presented are the *flap* and *shuffle*. Throughout your entire involvement with tap dance, these steps will always remain challenging, and they will probably be the hardest to master.

Flaps are now incorporated into the walk. This basic and essential step includes two tap sounds and is described as a brush-step. (See Figures 1.1–1.3.) Using the ball of the foot, the brush forward (brushing the foot away from the body) is the first sound of the flap and is executed with ease and a particular looseness of the entire leg. Many dancers advise beginning with the leg lifted and the knee bent (in front of the body) rather than having the leg

1.1

1.2

straight. Bending the leg from the onset will allow for a fuller, richer sound. If you start the flap with a straight leg (sometimes known as a nerve flap), the tone will not be as full. Starting with a bent leg is also easier on the knees and creates less tension in the leg. The step, the second sound of the flap, entails placing the ball of the foot on the floor while leaving the heel lifted. The accuracy of the placement can be marked by noticing the creases in the shoes, which are due to the lifted heel and the body weight concentrated on the ball of the foot.

Begin the exercise slowly, maintaining the same tempo for a while, and later, the time can be doubled, tripled, or performed as quickly as possible. It is essential that the dancer maintain the starting tempo for a designated time without rushing it or racing. As the step becomes more familiar, there is a tendency to increase the tempo, but this is incorrect. If one starts out doing thirty-two flaps at a slow pace, the tempo should be maintained for the entire count, then stopped and increased.

It is appropriate to mention the importance of the flap at this point. The flap is an integral part of the

1.3

Figures 1.1, 1.2, 1.3
The flap begins with a lifted knee and entails two tap sounds. The first tap sound is made by brushing the foot away from the body. The second sound is made by placing the ball of the foot on the floor with the body weight concentrated there and the heel lifted.

foundation of tap and is vital to any tap dance. In executing a flap, one must be concerned with clarity and precision. If these points are emphasized throughout early training, the dancer will have a better opportunity to internalize this information and, as a result, be a better dancer.

The second exercise, the shuffle, consists of a brush forward away from the front of the body and a brush back toward the body, using the ball of the foot to make the tap sounds. With a relaxed leg, the ball of the foot brushes forward and back, making a tap sound in either direction (see Figures 1.4–1.6.). This is practiced on one side at a time and then from side to side. In order to change from side to side, however, it is necessary to add a step on the ball of the foot, making it a shuffle-step. This also includes a weight change because as soon as you add the step to the shuffle, the body weight is transferred to the foot that produced the step. The entire shuffle-step is performed on the ball of the foot, especially when accommodating faster tempos. At the slower tempos, the entire foot may be placed on the floor after the shuffle so that balance can be maintained.

1.4

1.5

Separation of the toes and heels is important to note. Experiment by drumming with just the heels, then just the toes, going from left to right at various rhythms. When using only the heels, the torso is in a sitting position, and the knees are bent. Using only the toes, the knees remain bent, but the torso straightens and comes slightly forward. This is followed by toe-toe-heel-heel, performed either by leaving both feet on the floor or by lifting the foot off the floor for the toe-toe part, as though stepping up stairs. Because the feet are working close to the floor, these two exercises augment their speed. They also help establish the memory in the feet as to the actual proximity of the floor. You can then try standing on one leg and lifting either the toe or the heel of the standing leg to make a tap sound. This requires good balance and a sense of how your body actually manipulates.

These movements provide the foundation for the *cramp-roll*, a well-known tap step that entails placing the toes and heels individually on the floor (toe-toe-heel-heel), making four distinct tap sounds in rapid succession or in a roll. (See Figures 1.7–1.10.). As though walking up stairs,

1.6

Figures 1.4, 1.5, 1.6
The shuffle is a brush forth and back, making a tap sound in both directions.

1.7

1.8

1.9

1.10

Figures 1.7, 1.8, 1.9, 1.10
Toe-toe-heel-heel.

place the right toe, then the left toe on the floor, making one tap sound per toe. Leaving both toes in place, the heels are dropped (right heel-left heel). As the step becomes familiar, the pace increases, and you can try to roll the four taps. A small hop or lift is added to accommodate the tempo. Now reverse the exercise by starting with the left toe.

10

Brush-Toe-Heel The combination of steps for brush-toe-heel is important for movement because it can be danced either forward, backward, or sideways. The actual exercise consists of a flap and a heel, both done on the same foot. (See Figures 1.11–1.16.) It is easier to begin by going forward, using as much space as possible, and then practicing that same series of steps going backward. It improves your agility to move in different directions, using as much space as possible. Going to the left and right sides, however, requires the use of the hips.

The incorporation of hip movement is essential if you are to truly master the form, and this particular exercise is extremely useful in presenting the necessity of hip action. When moving toward the right with the brush-toe-heel step, the left hip juts toward the left when the right foot leads the movement. Similarly the right hip is positioned to the right when the left foot is doing the action. What occurs is a side-to-side swaying of the hips, and this allows the exercise to flow with considerable ease. The importance of relaxed, controlled hip movement cannot be stressed enough and should be noted in the early stages of tap instruction.

Figures 1.11, 1.12, 1.13, 1.14, 1.15, 1.16
Brush, toe-heel, right then left.

1.11

1.12

1.13

1.14

1.15

1.16

HELPFUL HINTS TO BEGINNERS

Dress. Your clothing should be as comfortable as possible. Leotards, tights, sweat pants, or baggy clothing are appropriate. You will be working up a bit of a sweat, and you wouldn't want to soil something good.

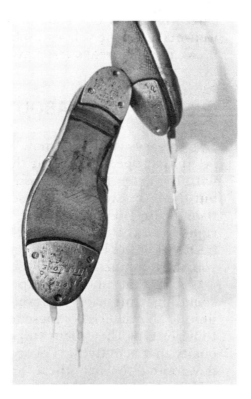

Shoes. The beginner may not want to invest in costly shoes (and tap shoes are), so look around for a pair of leather shoes that fit properly. The shoes should fit snuggly, and you should make sure that there is not too much space between the tip of your toe and the tip of the shoe. Providing that the shoe fabric is leather, the shoes will expand somewhat with the foot, although at times your feet may expand a great deal. Toe and heel taps are available in most dance shops. Although variety is limited, we have found Telltone taps to be among the best. Be sure that the taps are screw-in, rather than nails, so you can adjust the tightness. You will probably have to bring the shoes to a cobbler to have the taps put on. In terms of the size and shape of the heel, some prefer a higher heel (in women's shoes), while others prefer a flatter, wider heel, as found in men's shoes. The choice is yours, although the shorter flat heel allows for better balance and a fuller sound. When you do decide to make a shoe purchase, shop carefully in various shoe and dance shops and look for well-made leather shoes. Soft leather is always easier to break in and wreaks less havoc on the feet.

ABOUT TAP

"It's so easy when you know how," says Bubba Gaines, as he jumps rope and taps at the same time. And so it goes with the art of tap. Once you have the step, it seems easy, but the in-between stage of seeing and hearing a step and then trying to reproduce it can vary tremendously. So, right from the start, try not to think too much. Do your best, enjoy the learning process, and wait a while before you start competing with yourself.

A special quality of tap dance comes to mind. After spending time with the veterans of tap, we noticed a unique characteristic: these folks never get bored with the topic of tap. They seem to possess a pure and rare curiousity that is undying. Regardless of the many years spent developing the art, these pros always seem inquisitive when the conversation comes to tap. The enthusiasm of these dancers, coupled with the fact that they continue to perform, leaves them with a youthful quality, a delightful side effect of the form.

MUSIC AND TAP

Any discussion of tap, or any dance for that matter, is incomplete without the inclusion of its relation to music. Music and dance have a special relationship, which varies somewhat according to the dance medium you are talking about. When it comes to tap dance, we think of jazz, bebop, and swing. In actuality, you can tap to just about any kind of music, as long as you can keep the time and keep it well. It is also important for dancers to comprehend musicality, so that they will be able to converse with musicians when necessary.

Music is divided up into measure, with each measure having an equal number of beats or counts. The beat is the pulse, and its number depends on what is known as the music's time signature. For example, ¾ times means that there are three beats to a measure, like waltz time, whereas ¼ time means that there are four beats to a measure. For the most part, ¼ time is most common. In terms of dance, a measure signifies the division of the dance steps into periods of duration that correspond with the music.

In tap dance, we often discuss single, double, and triple time. What this means is that when you tap your foot in single time, you tap a count per beat, right on the beat, such as 12345678. When you count in double time, you count two sounds for each beat. For ¼ time, you would have one count on the beat and one count in between the beats, so you would count 1 and 2 and 3 and 4 and 5 and 6 and 7 and 8. Finally, when you count in triple time, there are three sounds for each beat or twenty-four counts for each two measures, counted 1 and a 2 and a 3 and a 4...

Listen to all kinds of music and try to determine the time of the particular tune. Clap the time out for a while and then try tapping. Stick with the basic time at first. Try to avoid becoming too fancy or filling the space with too much sound. Simplicity is preferable. Remember, silence is also a valid way to fill a space.

LEON COLLINS

"Dancing is the poetry of the body as music is the poetry of the soul," says Leon Collins. Born in Chicago, Illinois, Leon wanted to be a prize fighter and never really gave

dancing a thought. At the age of thirteen, Leon realized he had to make a choice, and after some formal training, he began dancing on street corners and in bars. Although amazed by Baby Lawrence, Leon claims that it was his training as a musician that influenced his work in tap dance. Inspired by Charlie Parker, Leon reproduced with his feet whatever Parker played on his horn. Part of his professional experience was playing guitar for the Three Dukes, and he later went on to perform tap dance in the U.S. and Europe with Honi Coles, Bubba Gaines, Charles Cooke, and Buster Brown, as well as solo. Leon currently teaches tap at Harvard and at Boston University, and in addition to performing, he maintains a dance studio in Boston.

Leon believes that tap is music, that we use our feet to get the same sound as an instrument. In addition to listening as accurately as possible, Leon feels that we must learn everything equally on both sides of the body. "Nothing is impossible because you have two feet," he remarks, and he invariably makes up combinations that go from one side to the other, using hand claps to fill in spaces. He feels that there is an advantage in dancing to music exactly as it is written, and he believes that improvisation is extremely important. "We must learn to dance to anything, even if the tempo is odd."

In terms of teaching, he finds it essential to truly reach the person you are trying to instruct, even if it takes doing the simplest walking step. Teaching dance is his practice, and Leon teaches each student personally. His success is obvious; students come from all over to study with him, and the love and rapport that exist in his studio are evident. Ages range from three to eighty-one, and any observer can see that the information is being passed on to all of the enthusiastic recipients. "I teach, the students learn, and I learn from the students." Leon speaks highly of his students, and he generously shares his life's work with all of them. Most remain a part of his life even after they decide to branch off in other directions.

On a more personal note, Leon confides that he tries to duplicate a sound the minute he hears it. If he cannot reproduce it, he goes right into the studio and practices. "I dance to keep in shape," says this lithe hoofer, "not to show off." About his career, Leon humorously states, "I've never had a bad write-up, but I'm not bragging because I'm not dead yet." Somehow it seems unlikely that this skilled, heartfelt dancer will ever receive an unkind review.

The Beginning

Tap dance is a wonderful adventure in learning. It not only provides you with the opportunity to learn rhythm, coordination, and body movement, it pronounces the complexities involved in developing equal control on both sides of the body. Most of us favor one side of the body and go through life habitually favoring the more adept of the two. Interestingly enough, this becomes a handicap, for then we never use the full capacities of our bodies. The study of tap dance, or any dance or sport, makes this peculiarity evident. You realize that one side of your body learns much faster, while the other side learns painstakingly slowly. This is a common malady among those who try to develop a skill that involves the entire body. Developing an equivalence between the right and left side of the body is a slow process, but it can be a successful and extremely useful experience.

This knowledge of body movement and the capacity for coordination is helpful. People of our time have become increasingly conscious of their bodies and what is necessary for their maintenance. Throughout the last two decades, there is more awareness of the numerous activities that improve the heart and overall muscle tone. Jogging, aerobics, walking, dance, tennis, hiking, racketball, skiing, and so many other activities have become devoted pastimes for those wishing to improve the condition of their overall health. The reason for this resurgence in physical activity is multifaceted, yet it stems partly from the fact that the human body is designed for great physical achievement. With the prominence of sedentary occupations, this rebirth not only holds physical importance, but mental and spiritual as well, and it is known that physical activities have strong therapeutic effects.

What is uniform among all these arts and activities is that they demand total presence of mind in order to be properly executed. In turn, this allows you to become fully absorbed and concentrated. The accumulation of skills and technique allows you the freedom to grow and be creative, and ultimately that is part of the goal. Another important factor is that, as much as possible, you should try to enjoy the experience of learning an entirely new language. It's a wonderful, challenging adventure, and as Steve Condos has commented, "Whenever I would work out by myself for a couple of hours, I would come out of the studio and walk the streets and my feet would feel like feathers. It felt so good just to walk." What a luxury to have that feeling available to us.

Begin this session by doing some stretches to loosen up the muscles and warm the body. Go nice and easy, so you don't place undue strain or tension in the body. You are trying to free the circulation and musculature, not bind it. After the exercises begin, warm up the feet by doing flaps and shuffles at various tempos, making sure the sounds are clean and crisp. Work on all the exercises given in the previous session in preparation for the new material that will be introduced.

Shuffle-Toe-Heel The exercise called shuffle-toe-heel produces four tap sounds, done on one foot at a time (see Figures 2.1–2.4). Practice this on the left foot first, balancing the body weight on the right; then switch. The step itself consists of a brush away from the front of the body, a brush toward the body, then the body weight is placed on the ball of the foot, and consequently, the heel is dropped, with each step consisting of one tap sound. As you become more comfortable with the step, try shifting from side to side. As the pace increases, a hop or a lift can be incorporated to make

22

Figures 2.1, 2.2, 2.3, 2.4
Shuffle-toe-heel.

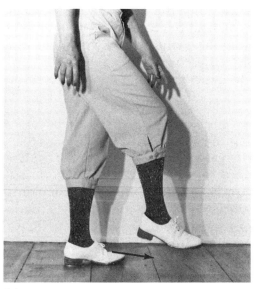

2.1

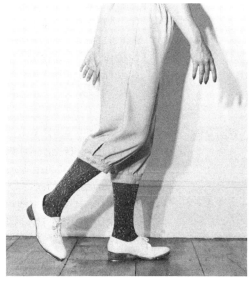

2.2

2.3

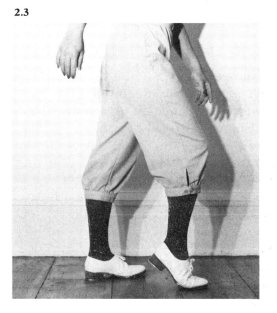

2.4

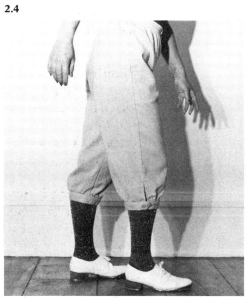

the weight change cleaner. This step then can be lengthened by first adding a heel on the left. You can later add a third heel on the right, making the step shuffle-toe-heel (right foot), heel (left foot), heel (right foot). The later two exercises are repeated on the same foot, as they do not allow side-to-side action, yet both provide an excellent opportunity for one to develop rapid, close-to-the-floor footwork.

Paddle and Roll This is a well-known tap step that is frequently used in routines. It entails a brush (toward the front of the body)-toe-heel on one foot and a dig with the heel of the other foot, making four tap sounds. Several things are important to note in this step: (1) the brush toward the body is made by snapping the ball of the foot on the floor, with brisk action; (2) the second heel, called a dig, is actually made by digging (not too roughly) the heel, quite different from dropping the heel; and (3) it is important to know where the accent is because brush-toe-heel-dig has a different accent than dig-brush-toe-heel. Again, we have weight shifts to concentrate on. Try to remember some of these points as you learn the step, and as usual, begin at a comfortable, easy pace so that you can manage the four taps per roll.

Riffs The final exercise for this session is called a *riff*, a walking step that includes either four or five tap sounds. The *four-noted riff* is done on one foot at a time and is comprised of a toe-heel-heel-toe, with the first two sounds made by carefully brushing the toe and heel against the floor while the second heel and toe are placed firmly on the floor, shifting the weight temporarily to that foot and freeing the other. The second kind of riff, or *five-noted riff* (see Figures 2.5–2.9), incorporates both feet and goes as follows: toe-heel (right), heel (left), heel-toe (right). To repeat, both of these riffs are walking steps and are rarely done in place. Try to feel relaxed in the arms and legs and take regular steps, making the tap sounds nice and even, and allowing the arms to move in a natural way (opposition: right arm, left leg).

24

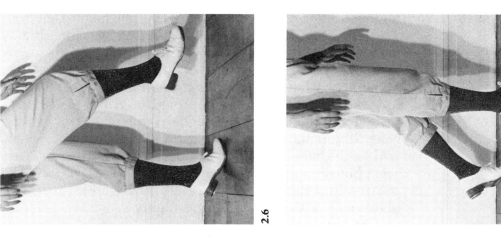

2.6

2.9

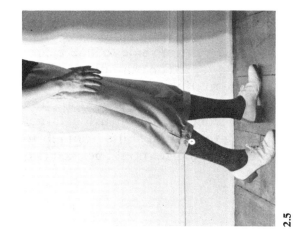

2.5

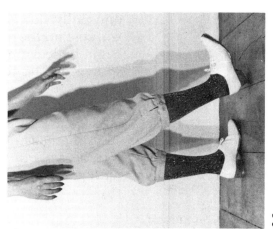

2.8

Figures 2.5, 2.6, 2.7, 2.8, 2.9
Five-Tap Riff: A walking step that entails five tap sounds. The first two tap sounds are a brushing of the toe and heel of the right foot, dropping the heel on the left and then placing the heel and toe of the right foot on the floor to make the two last tap sounds.

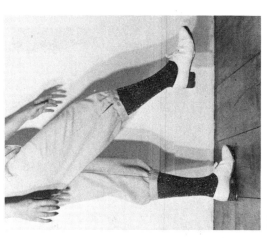

2.7

Tea for Two   Figures 2.10–2.49 illustrate the well-known soft-shoe routine Tea-for-Two. This classic routine was originally performed without taps and was highlighted by its grace, style, and beautiful lines rather than the taps themselves. It can be danced on the ball of the foot or flat-footed, and it has been performed innumerable times and ways throughout the years. This standard thirty-two-bar routine generally includes thirty-two bars divided into four parts with eight bars each, each bar devoted to a different step. The photos on pages 26 through 41 show the details of the routine and depict as accurately as possible the exact placement of this complex and highly syncopated dance.

The style of dancing in this particular routine is what makes it such a novelty. It has often been performed at an unusually slow pace, which requires incredible balance as you sustain the movement. In learning the routine, you can begin by learning the movements from side to side before you even start to include the taps. For example, without the taps, the beginning of the routine would be: step to the right with the right foot, cross front with the left foot, and then step right. You would concentrate on using larger steps than usual and making the weight shifts from left to right as smooth as possible. The dance should be executed with grace and ease.

Figures 2.10, 2.11
The way we depicted the style of the soft shoe is on the ball of the foot. Begin the routine with a flap on the right. Body weight shifts to the right foot.

2.11

2.10

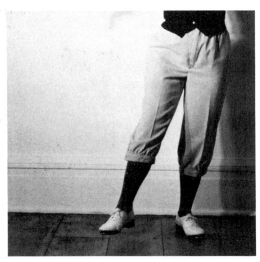

Figures 2.12, 2.13
Flap with the left foot as it crosses in the front of the right. Body weight shifts to the left foot.

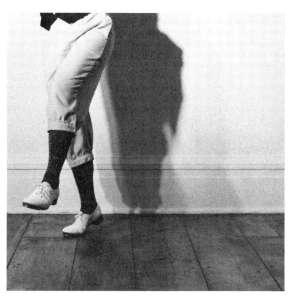

2.12

2.13

Figure 2.14
Step by placing right foot on floor
for one tap sound.

Figures 2.15, 2.16
Flap left.

2.15

2.16

Figures 2.17, 2.18
Flap right as you cross right leg in front of left.

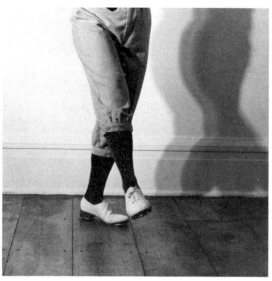 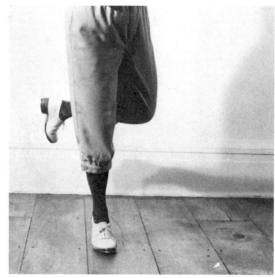

2.17

2.18

Figure 2.19
Step with left.

Figures 2.20, 2.21
Flap right.

2.20

2.21

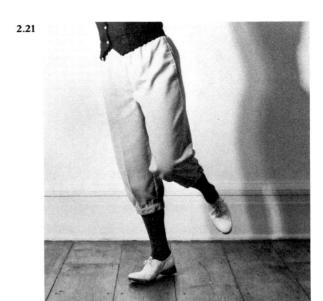

Figures 2.22, 2.23, 2.24
Flap left, step right.

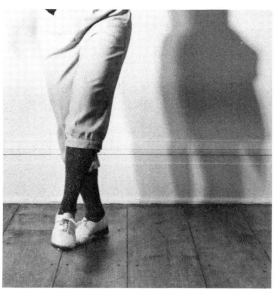

2.22

2.23

2.24

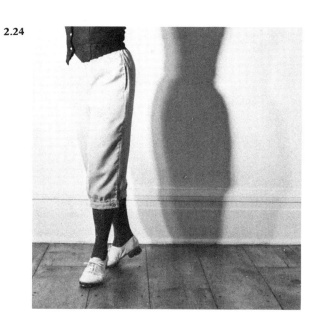

31

Figures 2.25, 2.26, 2.27
Brush back, toe left, step right.

2.25

2.26

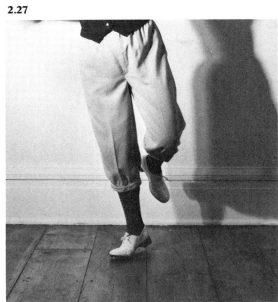

2.27

Figures 2.28, 2.29, 2.30
Brush-toe left, step right.
Repeat entire first section to the left.

2.28

2.29

2.30

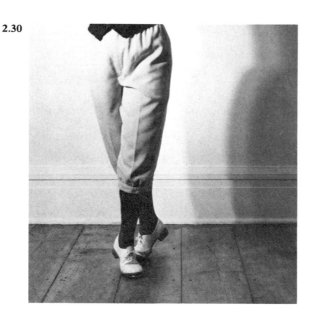

Figures 2.31, 2.32
Hop-step left.

2.31

2.32

Figures 2.33, 2.34
Step out right, cross back with the left.

2.33

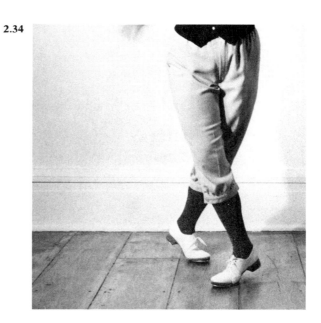

2.34

35

Figures 2.35, 2.36
Step out with right, cross front with left.

2.35

2.36

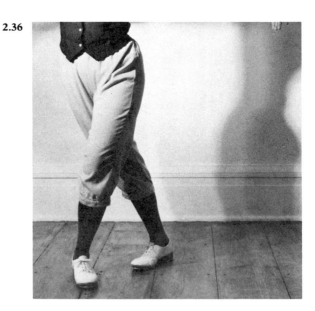

Figures 2.37, 2.38
Step out right, cross back left.

2.37

2.38

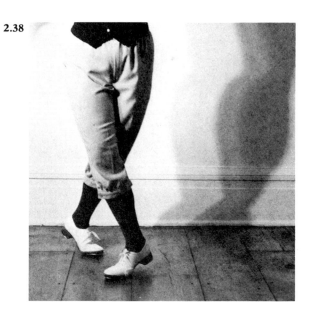

Figures 2.39, 2.40
Brush-toe right.

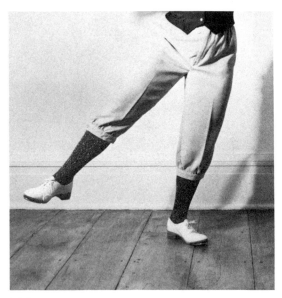

2.39

2.40

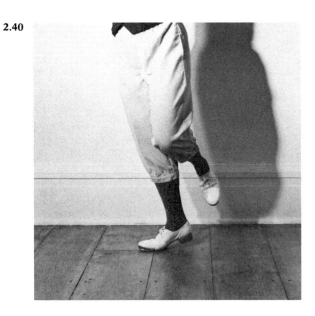

Figures 2.41, 2.42, 2.43
Brush-toe left, step right.

2.41

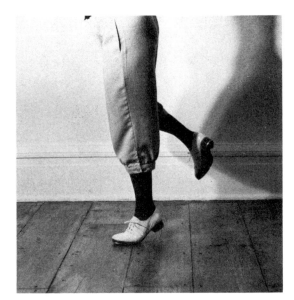

2.42

2.43

Figures 2.44, 2.45, 2.46
Brush-toe left, step right.

2.44

2.45

2.46

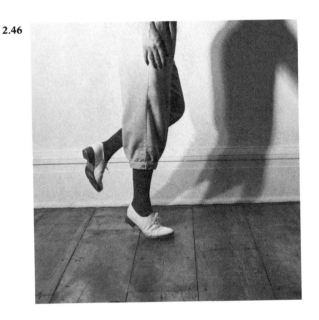

Figures 2.47, 2.48, 2.49
Brush-toe left, step right. Repeat this step with a hop on the right.

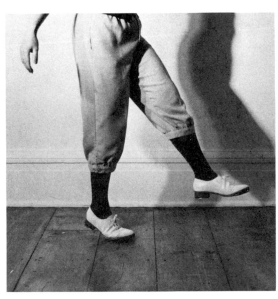

2.47

2.48

2.49

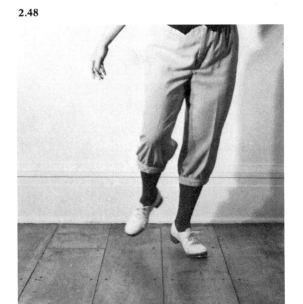

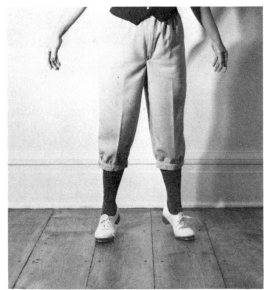

41

CATHY HARRIS

A thin, delicate child, Cathy Harris began tap dancing because her doctor suggested that it would improve her health. As fate would have it, Cathy became skilled quickly, and she was hired at a very young age by Benny Davis, who had a revue called *School Days*. She later traveled all around the country in vaudeville acts, performing in several top-notch theaters. The shows all had sixteen chorus girls, and Cathy would be the specialty act. She tenderly recalls performing with Bill Robinson at the Hippidrome in Baltimore. The following day, a review came out in the papers in which Robinson said that the only difference between himself and Cathy was that he had bigger feet.

Cathy's specialty was acrobatic toe tap in which she performed back flips, hand springs, nip-ups, and the likes on toe. "It was very dangerous because you never knew how you were going to land. My mother was always in the audience praying." Perhaps the most difficult feat that she performed was at the Roxy, where she danced toe tap on ice. For this occasion, special shoes were made that had nails placed in the soles, allowing Cathy to do cartwheels and roundoffs on the ice.

Realizing how strenuous and treacherous acrobatic toe tap was, Cathy switched to regular tap dancing. She became the Old Gold Girl on the "Ted Mack Amateur Show." "Ted always had some pros in with the amateurs," and Cathy worked all over, since the show flew to a different city each week. "Ted Mack was a good guy," says Cathy, "and I enjoyed working with him." She continues to perform with her daughter, doing impersonations of several of the great tap-dancers, and she teaches daily at Fazil's Dance Studio on 47th Street in Manhatten, where she has taught for over twenty years.

Cathy finds that most of her students become her friends. "You need patience for teaching, and if you see someone with two left feet, you can't get upset." Her method of teaching goes like this: "First I teach without music. I give them eight bars and see how good they are going to be. Then I always start off with a basic soft shoe, eight bars of "Tea for Two." I see if they have any rhythm and go on from there. I wait a while to teach a time step because they are not so easy. I follow this with a military routine and move on to advanced material like wings and pull backs. I teach audition material, such as the Grapevine, which is a soft shoe and a basic single time step. I really like to teach, but teaching can't be for everyone. When I see my students progressing and getting the material, it makes me happy."

Cathy finds the younger generation of tap-dancers a

terrific lot. "They are great because they are dedicated. They rent rooms and practice for hours. They perform everywhere, they even do acts on the streets in the summer. You have to be someone if you work that hard. You know, tap is the greatest because it is fun and it is here to stay; don't let anyone tell you any different."

3
Improvisation

You have been attending a class for three weeks and have begun to learn the rudiments of tap dance. It's much harder than you ever imagined, but you have decided to stick with it and accept the challenge. As you consistently confuse your left foot with your right, you wonder how those professionals make it look so easy. You have acquired a new reverence for dancers, tap-dancers in particular. You begin to realize that in order to make it look so easy, one must make a concerted effort to be conscious and devoted.

The instructor suggests that the group begin experimenting with improvisation. Each person will take a designated amount of time to perform some impromptu steps that correctly overlay the set rhythm. "Me?" you exclaim to yourself. "I couldn't possibly know enough to improvise!" "Yes, you," responds some knowing voice. "Use anything to make a sound—snaps, claps, taps, flaps, anything. Listen to the syncopation of the set rhythm and try to fill a bar with sound as simply and creatively as possible." With a bit of reluctance, you decide to give it a try.

Part of the reason people hesitate at improvisation is because they so fear making a mistake or not doing something "perfectly" from the beginning. That attitude, coupled with a lack of confidence, is often what prevents us from becoming creative and spontaneous with a new art. Perhaps what we have to reevaluate in ourselves is the childlike quality that allows us to be bold and remain unconcerned with the way others may possibly judge us. However, the primary attribute for spontaneity is a genuine ability to concentrate. Interestingly enough, what inhibits our capacity for concentration is the endless mind chatter that gets involved with doing things correctly or perfect. In this process, we also forget to apply what we have learned. Our focus should be geared toward developing concentration and applying our knowledge to the fullest. When that is finally achieved, something like improvisation becomes second nature.

Spending time in conversation with dancers and musicians, you learn that improvisation and creativity are a must. Accumulation of technique is surely a bonus, but technical growth should progress alongside creative growth. As you may well know, you need instant creativity in order to improvise. Improvisation requires on-the-spot ingenuity or "inventive talent." Having good technique is not sufficient: one must learn to be creative with that particular information in order to really "cut" the step. So, from the start, incorporate improvisation in the study of any art, particularly tap. Try not to be too fancy or complex; simplicity is always beautiful and appropriate. Use this as an opportunity to express yourself.

A group improvisation exercise can be done with or without music, provided time is kept in some fashion with the feet, hands, or voice. (When you improvise alone, use music or have something keeping time.) Each person takes two bars of the set time for improvisation.

Obviously the most important thing is to keep time accurately and to go from one person to the next without missing a beat. With practice, this becomes easier and more enjoyable. Employ different tactics to make improvisation appealing: use different musical concepts, change the lighting, perform with the eyes shut. Progress will occur rapidly if you are inventive. From here on, some part of every session should include improvisation.

Warm-up exercises should consist of several counts of flaps, shuffles, and steps that allow you to use large areas of space. These steps are helpful because you become accustomed to tapping and moving at the same time. It is nice to work in place but equally as important to use space. Just repeating toe-heel on alternating feet and taking as large a step as possible will limber up the body and accustom it to the combined action of stepping and making sounds. The bursh-toe-heel exercise in every direction is also an excellent way to use space. This is also useful for warming up the hips. This can be followed by riffs, which are a good walking step and can be performed in a circle. Paddle and roll (brush-toe-heel-dig) on alternate sides, starting slowly and then increasing the pace, comes next. This teaches exact proximity of the floor and trains the foot for rapid movement.

49

The exercises to be introduced next (Figures 3.1–3.11) are composed of the basic flap and shuffle, but in combinations that include a jump. Both are vigorous and require stamina. But your primary concern should be staying light on your feet so you can easily pick up your own weight. Start each step slowly, and try to increase the pace, and stay primarily on the ball of the foot.

Flap Shuffle Hop

Flap right
Shuffle left
Hop right

Flap Shuffle

Flap right
Shuffle left

Brush-Toe-Heel

For *brush-toe-heel*, the working foot is in a turned-out position, with the toe off the floor and some weight placed on the heel. As the toe is returned toward the body, the brush sound is made. Then the body weight is placed on the ball of the foot to make the second tap sound, and the heel is dropped for the third sound. The foot swings out to the side again via the heel, simply by lifting the front of the foot, leaving only the heel on the floor. This step is helpful in developing sideway flexibility of the foot. The very nature of the step and how it is executed is somewhat contrary to the way the foot usually moves, and it increases the suppleness of the foot.

Time Step

The *time step* evolved from a simple version of the vernacular dance step called the *buck*. The buck, which incorporated the shuffle and tap, was effectively changed in the early 1900s by a fine dancer, King Rastus Brown. The history on Brown is scant, but it is known that he revolutionized the buck into the time step and eagerly shared his innovation with the world of tap. Hence, the time step was assimilated into the repertoire of tap steps. Often used to set time, dancers frequently began their act

50

Figures 3.1, 3.2, 3.3
Flap.

3.1

3.2

3.3

Figures 3.4, 3.5
Shuffle.

3.4

3.5

Figures 3.6, 3.7
Hop.

3.6

3.7

Figures 3.8, 3.9
Flap.

3.8

3.9

Figures 3.10, 3.11
Shuffle very snappy.

3.10

3.11

53

with a time step in order to synchronize the music with the dance or to establish the tempo with other dancers. Noted for their unusual syncopation, time steps exist in a number of varieties. Dancers will often have original versions that they use as part of their act. Standard renditions have survived through the years and are now considered classics. Within this group is the well-known time step, Thanks for the Buggy Ride, which can be danced as a single, double, triple, or double-triple time step.

The actual body movement of the steps entails a sort of rocking forward and backward with little movement to the sides. When danced slowly, the movements can be easily exaggerated so that anyone doing the step for the first time will be able to understand the action and direction of the step. The accompanying photos depict the single and the actual tilt of the step. Thanks for the Buggy Ride (see Figures 3.12–3.19) is a mnemonic contrivance used for remembering the step and where the accents occur. Mnemonic devices exist for each version of this time step.

**And Thanks for the Buggy Ride
(Double Time Step)**

Brush right

Heel left

Flap right

Flap left

Step right

Step left

**And Thank You for the Buggy Ride
(Triple Time Step)**

Brush right

Heel left

Shuffle-step right

Flap left

Step right

Step left

And When Will We Take the Buggy Ride?
(Double-Triple Time Step)

Brush right

Heel left

Shuffle-step right

Shuffle-step left

Step right

Step left

Figure 3.12
Starting position with right leg
slightly in front of left.

Figure 3.13
Brush back with right foot
lift the left heel.

55

Figure 3.14
Drop left heel.

Figure 3.15
Step back with right.

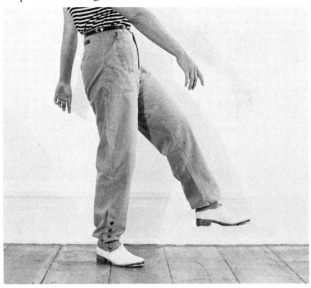

Figures 3.16, 3.17
Flap left.

3.16

3.17

57

Figure 3.18
Step right.

Figure 3.19
Step left, then repeat starting with a brush on the left.

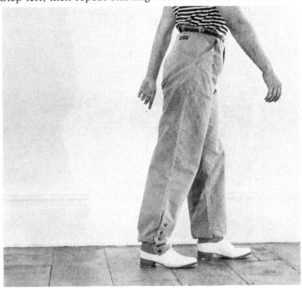

CHARLES "HONI" COLES

Charles "Honi" Coles began dancing at the age of twelve, strictly for recreational purposes. At that time, youngsters gathered on street corners during the summer months and held dance contests. Honi was fortunate enough to win a few amateur night contests at local Philadelphia theaters where he met George and Danny Miller. Although they never intended to dance professionally, they formed an excellent trio and danced wherever they could, which included the streets and local night spots. Their act at the time was a novelty one, entailing a stunt performed on pedastals approximately six feet high and one foot wide.

A show passing through town needed an act, and through a woman who knew the Millers, the trio was hired for a week in Norfolk, Virginia. This act led to another short gig in New York City at the Lafayette Theater, the leading black theater of the time. After a few short engagements and a lot of endless searching, Honi returned to Philadelphia and never worked with the Miller brothers again. The experience with the trio proved somewhat disappointing, but it provided an unusual stimulus for this dancer. Honi Coles went back to his hometown, cleaned out a room in his house, and proceeded to practice ten to sixteen hours a day for an entire year. "After that, I had the fastest feet in the business," states Honi. "I didn't say I was the best, but the fastest."

He returned to New York and played the Harlem Opera House and the Apollo Theater. He began to tour with several big bands and worked a great deal with Cab Calloway. Jobs were abundant during these years, and Honi's career continued to thrive. A position opened with the Lucky Seven Trio, a prominent dance group from California, and Honi performed with them throughout Europe and the United States for three years. He then performed solo, did a comedy act for three years, and worked again with Calloway. But it wasn't until after World War II that Honi teamed up with Charles "Cholly" Atkins to form the class act Coles and Atkins. Together they performed on Broadway in *Gentlemen Prefer Blondes*, in which they did all their own choreography and later toured with the show throughout the States. This job was followed by a European tour with Count Basie. Their success was renowned, and they continued to perform together until work became scarce during the late 1950s. The last of the great class acts, known for their beautiful adagio soft shoe, came to an end. Cholly became a choreographer for Motown groups, and Honi was offered the position of production manager for the Apollo Theater, where he stayed for several years. His tap-dancing career did not take off again until the mid-seventies when he was in the cast of the National Company of *Bubbling Brown Sugar*.

Honi speaks of the present as the most successful and satisfying period of his life, and he attributes this partially to the fact that he is relaxed. "Once you learn your trade, you learn to do it as easily as you possibly can, nice and easy with no big fat apparent effort. If you have done something for fifty years and can't do it easily, something is wrong." Although he prefers doing choreography, he still teaches privately and gives lecture demonstrations at colleges. He feels that the importance of his teaching is so that the art, as he interprets it, will survive. "In tap dancing, so many fine points are overlooked, like dynamics, for instance. There are soft periods and loud periods, it is not just banging." In teaching, Honi tries to convey the ease and naturalness; the centralization of the body; the subtleties of weight changes; how you lift your knee; the fine points of the art. "Tap has finesse, just as music does, because of the dynamics."

Watching Honi perform, it becomes clear why he is one of the most celebrated tap-dancers of the time. His ease and elegance give tap a wonderful dimension. His unsurpassed charm and charisma make all the people in the audience ardent fans of the art. The way he conveys and extends his accumulated history and knowledge wins you over immediately. We are indeed fortunate that this alluring gentleman endured and evolved with his art so he could continue to share it with us all.

4
Musicality

Brenda Bufalino at Jazzmania, New York, April 1982.

Most of us are born with a particular sense of musicality. Not necessarily the kind of musical genuius that produces a Mozart or Stravinsky, but a sense of speech, song, or movement, often manifestd in rhythmical patterns. We frequently observe in children an innate sense of rhythm, a natural ability to follow tempos, and a wonderful freedom with their bodies. Young people seem to hold on to that rhythm until various parts of the learning experience invade and cause a certain inhibition to occur. Outside of the arts and certain religions, the modern learning process can be a deterrent for the growth of our musicality and sense of rhythm.

Your involvement with tap dance will reestablish your relationship with rhythm and music. You begin to perform with your feet and body in much the same way as you would with an instrument. At the beginning level, you start with the basic steps (notes), such as flaps, shuffles, and paddles and rolls, just as you would learn musical scales. Through repetition and a keen ear, you learn to play these basic steps at just about any tempo, from the slowest to the fastest, providing, of course, that the sounds are clean. When the primary steps become more familiar, others are added and then combined to form routines (tunes), pretty sounds that adhere as perfectly as possible to the set time. As you progress, the tunes become increasingly more complex and demanding, but once your body has memorized the material, it becomes easy. Tap requires accurate interpretation and being "on top" of what is happening. It provides an excellent vehicle for the human body to become a musical instrument.

"Tap dance is a young art form that developed from people playing other people's rhythms, inserting their own creative line," says jazz musician Charlie Kniceley. Kniceley, who has accompanied several tap-dancers in concert, feels that they write their own music by taking simple melodic concepts and adding flavors to them. "Tap is primarily a swing idiom and tap-dancers should listen to swing. Choose a player that you really like and listen to him a lot because there is an endless amount of information available." Charlie finds that too much dissection is harmful because it can lead to a lack of feeling for the entire message. He also feels that improvisation is a must. As a teacher, he insists that his students begin immediately with improvisation because he finds it essential for growth. "You don't have to be an innovator to be creative. Take as much of the skill as you have accumulated and improvise with it. Even if it is one step or note, it can be played rhythmically in several different ways."

It cannot be reiterated enough that if you allow yourself to be inventive and creative with any endeavor, you will experience growth, a sense of enjoyment, and creative expression, none of which money can buy!

After the usual warm-up period (consisting of flaps, shuffles, etc., plus movements that take up lots of space), we will piece together two familiar exercises into one. Joined together are a five-tap riff, two paddle rolls, plus an end step that is a heel-brush on one foot and heel on the other. Both feet are kept pretty much under the hips because this exercise is designed to increase the speed of the feet and teach them the exact proximity of the floor. Begin this exercise slowly, attempting to get every sound out as clearly and cleanly as possible. Since very little body movement is required, it is easy to concentrate on the feet. Try to keep the syncopation even throughout the routine and avoid rushing the parts that come easier. For instance, the riff may be harder to dance, whereas the paddle and roll may be easier. Since the riff starts the combination, it sets the particular time of the routine, so be careful to follow the set time exactly. As the step becomes effortless, the timing can increase. Be conscious of clarity and cleanliness. At all costs, refrain from rushing.

Toe-heel right

Heel left

Heel-toe right

Heel-brush-toe-heel left

Heel-brush-toe-heel right

Heel-brush left

Heel right

Then repeat, beginning with the left side.

67

Second Time Step   Begin with a slow tempo. It starts with four brisk walks with one tap per step. When the initial step begins with the left foot, the fourth step on the right foot is followed by a brush toward the body, which is actually a "snap." Similarly, when you do the brush on the left foot, it is more like a snap toward the body. (See Figures 4.1–4.10.)

Figures 4.1, 4.2, 4.3, 4.4
Four steps forward starting with your left foot.

4.1

4.2

4.3

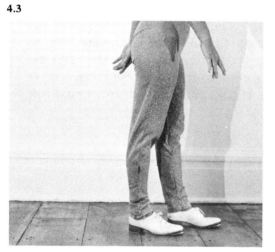

4.4

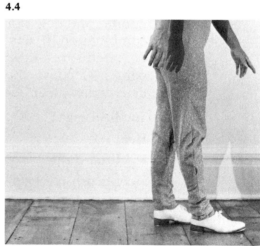

Figures 4.5, 4.6
Brush-step right.

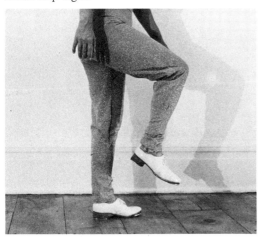

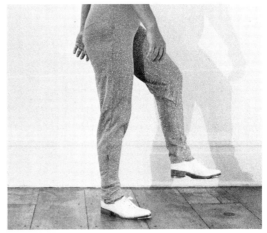

4.6

Figures 4.7, 4.8, 4.9
Step-brush-step.
on the left.

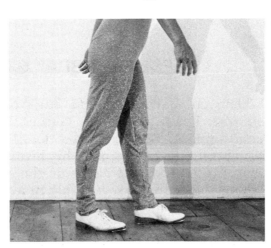

4.7

4.8

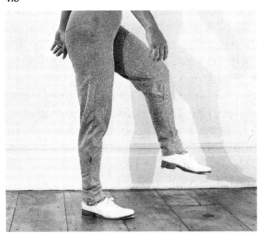

4.9

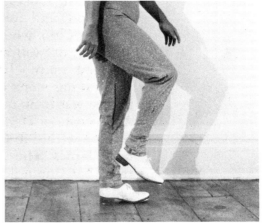

Figure 4.10
Step right. Then count 2–3–4 or do three flaps and start the exercise again starting with the same side.

LESLIE "BUBBA" GAINES

"When you reach your foot out, you gotta get there," remarks Leslie "Bubba" Gaines. A delightful conversationalist, Bubba speaks fondly of his life as he thoughtfully recaps some of his history. Bubba was initiated into the world of dance on the streets of New York. Here he danced with several big time fellows who showed him the rudiments of the art. Inspired by the dancing of Sunshine Sammy, who starred in the *Our Gang* comedies, Bubba became serious about tap at the age of fourteen. He was influenced by many stylists, especially those he considered the most fluid dancers, such as Eddie Rector, Bill Robinson, and John Bubbles. He was introduced to the Hoofer's Club, where he met the famous tap group Tip Tap and Toe, as well as Bill "Bojangles" Robinson and later jammed in the back room with other young dancers, exchanging steps and challenging. Within a short time, Bubba was in an act called The Three Dukes, International Aristocrats of Dancing. They toured together throughout Europe with Cab Calloway and later on their own. It was from James "Hutch" Hudson, one of the members of the trio, that Bubba learned the rope, a flash act that entails jumping rope while tap dancing, which, as you can well imagine, is quite a vigorous feat.

"In those days, everyone had a bag of tricks. Everyone invented their own way of doing the various flash steps, such as Over the Top, wings, toe stands, flips, anything sensational." Challenges were also a big part of the act, much to the delight of the audience. The Three Dukes even had a military routine where they danced on top hats, a show stopper that was performed over, around, and on the hats. The group was performing in Europe when World War II errupted and was forced to return to the U.S. Bubba was immediately inducted into the service and returned to Europe, where he served with Patton's army. When the war ended, Bubba began doing a single for the USO and continued his travels all around the globe. For twenty

years, he worked with the legends of jazz in various continents performing his art with great style and elegance, pleasing audiences throughout the world. The last decade has proven to be a prolific period for Bubba Gaines. He has performed innumerable times as a member of the Copasetics. He continues to do a single act that brings him to various parts of the country, and in the last few years, has shown his material to his protegee, a young woman with whom he now performs.

"Tap is one of the toughest things there is," he states. "The more you mess with it, the more you realize how difficult it is. One must know the fundamentals of the art and the movements that make it all possible, in order to be a real good dancer. You should be able to see what someone is doing and reproduce it no matter how hard it is. If you expect to get good at tap, you have to master it. You must have the steps at your command so that whenever you move, it is there. In addition, a good dancer needs a strong left."

Since most of his career has been spent performing on the road, Bubba devoted little time to teaching. Recently, however, he has spent a good deal of energy showing his protegee his material. He has found this to be a very pleasant experience. "I can see myself in her. She does it like I used to and she is good because she has the stamina and youth, in addition to good technique and a strong left."

Bubba thinks the future of tap dance will be promising. "Tap is going to be big because the new generation is into it and they will push it. It is time to spread tap out, but for that you need good people, good dancers, and that doesn't happen overnight." He likens tap to any musical instrument. "You don't pick up a horn and have instant virtuosity, it takes time." Bubba has found that audiences love tap's vitality and life, and that it is appreciated all over the world as a universal language. Bubba's words of advice? "Work for it, it is well worth the effort. Then, once you get it and know how it is done, enjoy yourself."

Vaudeville

The dictionary definition of vaudeville states that it was chiefly U.S. theatrical entertainment consisting of a number of individual performances, acts, or mixed numbers such as singing, dancing, and gymnastics. The word itself was derived from the French "Chanson du Vau de Vire," a song about the Valley of Vire in Normandy.

Minstrels, which had been a well-liked form of entertainment in the U.S. during the mid-1800s, began to lose popularity after a few decades and gave rise to vaudeville. White vaudeville began in the early 1880s when a gentleman named Tony Pastor presented an eight-act show at the Fourteenth Street Theater in New York. The acts varied from song, comedy, and dance to acrobatics, and they were designed to be cheerful, amusing family entertainment. In vaudeville, tap dancing continued to develop and grow, producing several of the classic routines and flash steps, as well as some of the finest tap-dancers. It is said that the first stair dance was performed at this time by one of three people (Eddie Mack, Al Leach, or Margie Trainor). Off to Buffalo and Falling Off the Log were popularized by the great Pat Rooney, and later the Condos Brothers innovated the Five Tap Wing. Other great dancers of the time were James Barton, who did an imitation of black legomania; Harland Dixon, of the team of Doyle and Dixon, who perfected pantomime; and the legendary George M. Cohan, who began his multifaceted career in vaudeville.

The black counterpart of vaudeville, which began in the early 1900s, was called Theatre Owner's Booking Association, sometimes nicknamed Tough On Black Artists or T.O.B.A. This association booked black artists throughout the North and the South and was started by a man named Sherman Dudley. A leading act in T.O.B.A. was the Whitman Sisters, four sisters who ran a successful show for at least forty years. One sister, Alberta, was known as one of the best male impersonators of the time, and another sister, Alice, was billed as the best female tap-dancer. Alice's son, Albert "Pops" Whitman, later became one of the best acrobatic tap-dancers ever. With a keen eye for talent, the Whitman Sisters gave hundreds of young

76

people their first breaks and are spoken of highly even today. Other well-known performers of the time included King Rastus Brown, who was an expert buck dancer; Eddie Rector, known for his elegance and fluidity; and Dewey Weinglass, an expert Russian-style dancer.

Perhaps the best tap-dancer of vaudeville was Bill "Bojangles" Robinson (the name Bojangles is derived from *bone jangler*, a musician who beats out rhythm by knocking a pair of bones together). Born in Richmond, Virginia, Bill Robinson was a important figure in the advancement of vernacular dance. He started his performing career at the age of twelve and played vaudeville for nearly thirty years, dancing his way to the top. As vaudeville gave rise to Broadway, Robinson became Broadway's first black dancing star and was recognized by the media because of his superb talent. He was fifty years old at that time. Well-known for his stair dance, Bojangles revolutionized tap dance by bringing it up on the toes and producing beautiful rhythmic patterns. In 1932, Robinson went to Hollywood, and three years later costarred with Shirley Temple in *The Little Colonel*. Robinson enjoyed his reputation as a bad guy, yet many loved the man. He also boasted that he could run backward faster than most people could run forward, but the evidence for that is slim. "Everything is copasetic," he often said, a phrase that would live on in history.

Vaudeville began to fade in the 1930s, yet for many the memory of it extends well into the 1940s. The advent of story musicals and the increasing popularity and availability of television brought vaudeville to an end. But the memory lingers. As one octogenarian female saxophone player reflects, "It was a good way of life, lots of hard work, lots of shows, but I loved it."

An interesting exercise to begin class involves playing impromptu rhythm patterns with either the toes, the heels, or both. The student is then asked to repeat the pattern after hearing it once. For example, think of a particular song or rhythm and play it with only the heels. Still using the heels, tap out a similar tempo, changing the accents. Keep varying this, incorporating the toes and combining the toes and heels. Your memory and acumen will improve from this type of workout. Follow this exercise with flaps, shuffles, paddle and rolls, etc., danced in single, double, and triple time.

Let us go back to slow flaps. We are going to produce the same step with different parts of the tap, which in turn will produce different sounding flaps. Make a flap with the ball of the foot as it is usually done. Follow this with a flap made with the very tip of the toe tap. The former will have a firm, loud sound, while the latter will be softer with a higher pitched sound. Similarly, experiment with the inside and outside of the tap by doing shuffles to the side. Brush out, using the outside surface of the tap, and brush in by using the inside surface of the tap. Not only will the shuffle sound somewhat different, but the dancer will be exercising the foot in an alternate fashion. Experiment doing flaps and shuffles on the various parts of the toe tap and notice the different qualities and textures of sound. Also try executing flaps from every position around the body: front, side, crossing in front of and in back of the standing leg.

It is often said that mastering the art of turning is essential in perfecting the art of dance. "If you cannot turn, do not call yourself a dancer," is a frequently heard statement. Turning on taps is every bit as important. Spotting is the first thing one learns about turning. To spot, focus on anything that is at eye level and maintain that spot with the eyes as long as possible while the body begins to turn. When the eyes can no longer focus on the designated spot, the head whips around, and the eyes reestablish the focus on the same spot. You can practice turning to the right and to the left equally well by staying in place or by stepping forward, taking two steps per turn. As turning becomes effortless, flaps or brush-toe-heels take the place of the steps, and the speed of the turn is increased. It is important to reiterate that practicing on both sides is imperative. Always working to one side is a hindrance in dance and must be avoided.

Also introduced in this session are *pullbacks* (Figures 5.1–5.3) and *wings* (Figures 5.4–5.7). These steps are usu-

Figures 5.1, 5.2, 5.3
Pull back on one foot.

5.1

5.2

5.3

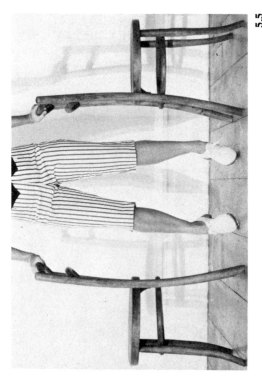

5.5

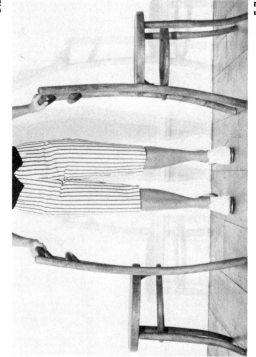

5.7

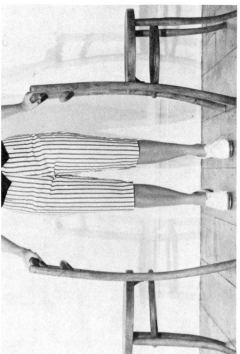

5.4

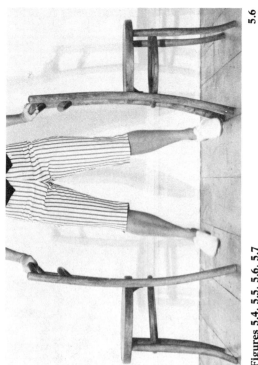

5.6

Figures 5.4, 5.5, 5.6, 5.7
A wing with both feet at the same time.

ally taught on a barre or with two chairs so that the student can get the feel of the step and still maintain balance. Afterward, the steps are performed without assistance. Due to the initial difficulty in mastering these steps, begin by using some means of support. Concentrate on making the body as light as possible while maintaining contact with the floor. These steps compel you to think up and down at the same time, an opposing concept at best. A pullback is two tap sounds and is almost like doing an air flap. It can be performed going forward or backward, as well as on one foot or two. To begin the exercise, start with both feet flapping back. Get the feel of lifting the body weight and landing on two feet simultaneously. Then experiment going back on only one foot and then try every combination of the step. If you have been using support up to this point, try the step without it. When you try to do a wing, use the support again and try doing a shuffle-step out to the side simultaneously using both feet. This exercise is extremely difficult, but if you keep at it, you will soon have results. Another variation on this step is to keep one leg bent and slightly out of the way while the standing foot does a shuffle-step to the side. These two steps are very demanding and require a good deal of practice. Don't be discouraged if it takes a while.

The routine presented in this section is called the Bill Robinson. Characteristic of the style of the man who made it famous, this routine is light and airy and is performed on the ball of the foot (Figures 5.8–5.16). It goes as follows:

Shuffle right

Hop left

Flap right

Flap left

Step right

The combination described in Figures 5.8 through 5.16 is repeated a total of six times alternating from the right side to the left. End the routine with the following break, repeated twice:

Step left (This step is somewhat like falling forward)

Shuffle-step right

Brush-toe-left (For the toe, the last tap of the break, cross back with the left foot.)

The toe on the last step of the break is almost like a pull back. Complete the break with a step on the left.

Figures 5.8, 5.9
Shuffle right.

5.8

5.9

Figures 5.10, 5.11
Hop and land on left.

5.10

5.11

Figures 5.12, 5.13
Flap right.

5.12

5.13

83

Figures 5.14, 5.15
Flap left.

5.14

5.15

Figure 5.16
Step right.

84

BRENDA BUFALINO

A prominent force in the resurgence of tap dance in recent years has been Brenda Bufalino. Raised among professional singers and musicians, Brenda began dancing at the age of four. She feels her interest in dance was sustained because there was always rhythm and music at home. Brenda describes her first dance teacher, Professor O'Brian, as a true disciplinarian who stressed precision and thoughtfulness. "This was a primary influence in my life, in my dancing and teaching." Brenda's early exposure to jazz dance and a different style of tap occurred in Boston at Stanley Brown's studio and later in New York with Honi Coles. "When I began studying with Honi, I really started to learn rhythms," she notes. Honi immediately became her mentor. Several years later she would perform with him.

As her proficiency in tap grew, work in the tap idiom became scarce. She was compelled to perform in other dance mediums, particulary Afro-Cuban and avant garde jazz. Early in the seventies, however, when few people were talking about tap, Brenda brought her old black cloth tap shoes to the dance studio and began to pass the art on to several young enthusiasts. From that time on, her involvement in tap began to increase at a phenomenal rate.

Along with Dorothy Anderson and several others, Brenda produced and directed the video documentary called "Great Feats of Feet" in 1975. The tape recounts the dance experiences of the famous Copasetics. In the documentary, several well-known routines are performed, and there are touching interviews that reveal the ups and downs of the careers of each dancer.

Brenda has performed throughout the U.S. and Europe and has often appeared as a guest lecturer in several colleges. Her performances have included ensembles, solo acts, and several partners, one of whom is Honi Coles. Together they successfully performed Morton Gould's *Tap Concerto*, an unusual composition that unites classical music and tap. She has also choreographed several shows and is an extremely competent writer.

Brenda had some interesting comments about teaching. "I never wanted to teach tap because I didn't feel it was a teachable subject. How do you teach rhythm tap?" Yet her life was full of dancers anxious to learn the art, so she began formulating and developing a technique for teaching and was very successful. "It became obvious to me that this form of dance was the most demanding, with the most scope. As a result, exercises matured that worked in rhythm and phrases. I began to consider the kinesiology of tap dance, realizing that it could never be just the feet. I began to recognize how sound comes from the whole body. It became apparent that movement was important in its relationship to what it could bring out of the feet."

Brenda feels that being a teacher has helped her understand exactly what she does because she must explain it to her students. "I wouldn't be a tenth as conscious if I didn't have to describe what it is I do." Brenda's teaching has also inspired her fascination with how the body moves to get the feet going and the taps out. "When taps come out because of movement and you bring the movement to accommodate the tap, then you have a style. With tap there is always a challenge ahead of you."

Hollywood

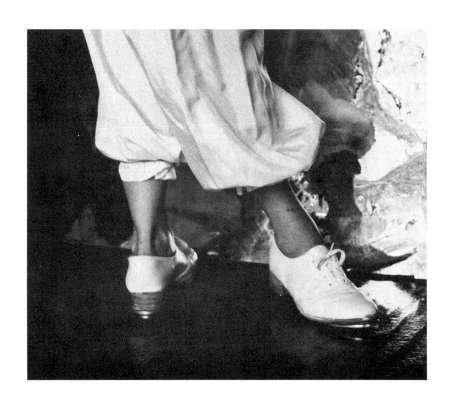

Imagine a vast land overlooking the Pacific Ocean, rather hilly to the north and equally flat to the south. The land itself is dry, often very dusty, and laden with fig trees, eucalyptus plants, and various types of cactus. At times, the land is farmed for semitropical fruit and peas. During periods of drought, however, the land is difficult to cultivate. The population is sparse, and the way of life is relatively peaceful. This briefly depicts southern California as it existed prior to the great migration to the West.

Upon moving to southern California in the early 1880s, a young woman named Daeida Wilcox requested that her wealthy husband build her a country estate. He obliged by buying a 120-acre parcel of land in the northwest corner of Los Angeles. Upon its completion, Daeida decided her home would be called "Hollywood," simply because she fancied the name. Her husband, H. H. Wilcox, later devised a plan for Hollywood, dividing it into rectangular parcels that would compose the posh community that he intended it to be. But plans often go awry, and H. H. Wilcox's dream fell short (in his estimation) upon arrival of the first film crew.

It was around 1903 that Thomas Edison invented and produced the first motion picture, *Uncle Tom's Cabin*. The concept was favorably received and before long the film industry began to blossom, particularly on the West Coast. In 1913, Cecil De Mille produced the first big feature film entirely filmed in Hollywood, *The Squaw Man*. The advent of sound in film occurred around 1927 in the Al Jolson movie *The Jazz Singer*, and as early as 1929, a large percentage of films included dance.

As American innovations, tap dance and motion pictures grew together in American entertainment. The first "talkie" to include tap dance was *Hollywood Revue of 1929*, starring Joan Crawford. Early dance routines used in musical films originated from the Broadway stage, yet they somehow lacked movement. Busby Berkeley is credited for his contribution in film movement because of his use of grand sets with enormous numbers of people. Popularity led to demand and soon people such as Bill Robinson and Fred Astaire starred in some of the most historically famous dance films ever produced in Hollywood.

Fred Astaire was born in Omaha, Nebraska, around the turn of the century. By the time he was six years old, he and his nine-year-old sister Adele were a major child act in vaudeville. They were a successful act for several years until Adele retired from show business. Fred continued on to a monumental career on stage and in films.

Astaire received much of his training at Ned Wayburn's Studio in New York where he learned to clog dance and reportedly was influenced by ballroom dancers Vernon and Irene Castle. He proceeded to combine the modes of tap, jazz, ballroom, and ballet into what he called his "outlaw" style. Astaire was a perfectionist in his trade and worked tirelessly so that each step he executed was absolutely precise. His unique style and elegance gained him tremendous popularity on stage and even more so in films. Astaire laboriously studied the process of photographing dance for the screen and was one of the few dancers who made their own tap sounds in film (Bill Robinson did also).

In several of his motion pictures, Fred Astaire had a female costar he danced and romanced throughout the film. The list of costars is elaborate and included some of the most famous actresses of the time. Undeniably, the most outstanding partner was Ginger Rogers. Through Astaire's influence and training, Ginger Rogers became known as a dancer. Together, this duo charmed millions of viewers as they skillfully portrayed romance in the nature of dance routines. Each of their ten films contains at least one ballroom duet for Fred and Ginger, and most often we find Fred trying to convince Ginger of his love. Grand sets, elaborate costumes, and artistic choreography gave the Astaire-Rogers partnership an unsurpassed charm and a certain timeless spirit.

Following is a list of some Hollywood performers who tap-danced in films:

Fred Astaire, *Broadway Melody of 1940*
Ray Bolger, *The Wizard of Oz*

93

John Bubbles, *A Star Is Born*

James Cagney, *Yankee Doodle Dandy*

Dan Dailey, *Give My Regards To Broadway*

Judy Garland, *Broadway Melody of 1938*

Ruby Keeler, *Forty-Second Street*

Gene Kelly, *Singing in The Rain*

Ann Miller, *Hit The Deck*

George Murphy, *For Me And My Gal*

Gene Nelson, *Lullaby of Broadway*

Nicholas Brothers, *Stormy Weather*

Donald O'Connor, *Yes Sir That's My Baby*

Eleanor Powell, *Ship Ahoy*

Bill Robinson, *Little Colonel*

Ginger Rogers, *Shall We Dance*

Shirley Temple, *Rebecca of Sunnybrook Farm*

Barrel Turn Following the customary warm-up, we will learn *barrel turns* (Figures 6.1–6.4). Begin by bending forward, leaving the head up, and maintaining a 90° angle with the body. Lift the right leg if you're turning toward the left (arms turn counterclockwise). When you finish turning, you are in the original starting position for this turn.

Over the Top *Over the top* involves jumping over your own leg. Bring the right leg in front of the left and rest the foot on the lateral side without placing pressure on the foot. Try jumping over the right leg, bringing the right leg behind the left leg in the end position (Figures 6.5–6.7).

Waltz Clog The *waltz clog* (Figures 6.8–6.17) is among the oldest of tap steps and was made famous by Pat Rooney and later Eddie Rector. A fairly vigorous combination, the waltz clog includes a major step that ends in a flash step (these two steps are repeated together three times) and ends in a break. It is danced in ¾ time signature and requires you to be rather light on your feet.

Figures 6.1, 6.2, 6.3, 6.4
Barrel turn.

6.1

6.3

6.2

6.4

Figures 6.5, 6.6, 6.7
Over the Top.

6.5

6.6

6.7

Figure 6.8
Step left.

Figures 6.9, 6.10, 6.11
Shuffle-ball right.

6.9

97

6.10

6.11

98

Figure 6.12
Step left.

Figure 6.13
Step right.

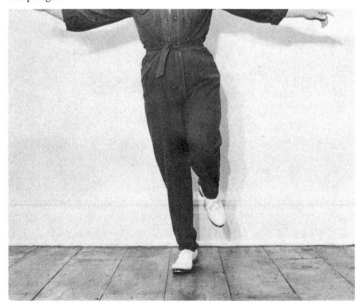

99

Figures 6.14, 6.15, 6.16
Shuffle-step left.

6.14

6.15

6.16

Figure 6.17
Step right.

101

Figures 6.8 through 6.17 are followed by a break:

Step left

Brush forward right

Hop left

Step right

Brush forward left

Hop right

STEVE CONDOS

"As a kid in south Philadelphia, all we did was dance. Dance in the streets, in the alleyways, anywhere. We used to go 'busking', on Broad Street, the main thoroughfare, and dance to collect pennies, nickels, and dimes. All the kids danced in that section. We also had access to the backstage of the Standard Theatre and saw all the great acts with all that beautiful music. I was determined that I was going to get on stage and dance."

So began the illustrious tap dancing career of a delightfully sincere and talented artist, Steve Condos. He received much of his dance training from his older brother Frank and was later highly influenced by James Barton, who Steve considers a prodigy of the theater. Frank taught Steve about music, how to practice, and inspired him to be creative. Frank and another brother, Nick, were already an established act called the Condos Brothers. Steve later replaced Frank in the team. "Frank was a genius, he knew about music, he had such beautiful rhythms," recalls Steve. Frank was also the creator of the Five Tap Wing, an extremely difficult step where one foot is kept in the air while the other foot is thrown out to catch five beats. Nick went on to perfect the step, incorporating it creatively in several of their performances. The Five Tap Wing became their acclaimed flash act since only they could perform the step.

The Condos Brothers (Nick and Steve) successfully continued their act for fourteen years, performing in all the major theaters and nightclubs throughout the country, working with the greatest swing bands of the era, such as Jimmy Dorsey, Tommy Dorsey, and Benny Goodman. They completed over twenty films, the best with 20th Century Fox, co-starring such people as Betty Grable, Sonja Henie, W. C. Fields, and Jane Powell. When the Condos Brothers split up, Steve immediately joined the Woody Herman Band as a guest artist, performing solo for the first time in his career. Without the time to make up routines, the Condos had to create something new for each show. Considering the caliber of the musicians, this was quite a feat. "I got encouragement and so-called style from being forced to do new things for every show."

Steve considers himself a musician (he plays piano, drums, and trumpet) as well as a percussive dancer. "I train my legs as a drummer trains his hands and hopefully get to the point technically where I can play anything that comes to mind." Always create, he advises the dancer. "It is easy to create or it gets easy as long as you practice." Focusing on his own rudiments of tap dance. Steve still practices and loves to dance. "I don't concentrate on routines because a routine is like an old cliche." If a step becomes a cliche, he changes it immediately by changing the accents and the beats, and then it becomes a new step. He received a wonderful opportunity to prove his virtuosity while performing in the Broadway production of *Sugar*. Realizing Condos' forte, director-choreographer Gower Champion did not restrict Steve's style by demanding a set routine, but allowed him the freedom to create anew at each performance. Steve remains ever grateful for this. For the two years that the show continued on Broadway, he tried to top himself each night and then continued with the same spirit in four different road versions of the show.

Steve feels that tap dancing is great for your health, and that you can start at any age; you don't have to be a young child to begin.

"It is a fun art," he claims, "not as set as other dance forms." He also finds that you can transfer your technique. For instance, if he applies his dancing technique to his acting, it works somehow. "When you have a certain technique in something, when you realize it, you can transfer it to do other things. What is interesting about tap is that the older you get, the better you get if you stick with it. I feel like I am getting better and better. Of course I can't jump around like I used to, but I don't want to anyway. Right now, I am in a rhythmical groove, like a drummer."

"If I had to do it all over again, I would do it the same way and definitely put in all the time I have. The kicks that

I have gotten from dancing and creating would be hard to duplicate in any other form of work. Plus, it keeps you young. There is no better exercise than dancing, any dancing. Thank God that I took the route I did, it proved beneficial. When things got a little rough, I would go to the rehearsal studio and dance for four or five hours and when I left, I had forgotten all my troubles. I would walk down the street and it felt so good to walk, my feet would feel like feathers."

Steve's advice for the dance enthusiast is to practice, practice, practice, and always be creative with the art. He feels the tap-dancer should practice with his feet and legs, the same as a drummer. "Don't use stress to obtain the movement, just go nice and slow. No matter what the rhythm, it will always act as a pump for the body, and the movement will evolve."

Filled with sincere love for dance and the dancer, Mr. Condos firmly states that tap dance will always be around. "There will always be someone in some corner of the earth developing rhythms with their feet that will lead to a style and technique that will astound people in the future. Today you have people studying all forms of dance who respect the rhythm value of tap. With their knowledge of their kind of music, there have to be a few geniuses out of that." Without a doubt, Steve Condos is a true inspiration, a fine example of a man filled with respect for life and art.

7

Body Movement

Body movement was the earliest form of communication. The body communicated by using the limbs, torso, hands, feet, and face. With the most natural and basic instrument available, early people used their bodies as vehicles for emotional expression, and in this fashion the earliest dances were created.

In many creeds, dance maintained an important sociological position and served as a spiritual form of communication with the deities. Reverence for nature and the gods was expressed via dance. In terms of healing, magical powers were and still are attributed to dance. In some cultures, healers dance to exorcise the evil spirits that inhabit the body of the sick. During the Middle Ages, people danced hysterically to avoid the plague, and in Italy, during the fifteenth and sixteenth centuries, it was believed that the bite of the Apulian spider caused tarantism, and that the cure was a tumultuous jumping dance which evolved into the tarantella. Throughout recorded history, it seems apparent that life could be somehow perpetuated through dance.

The structure of dance is composed of the most basic body movements, such as walks, leaps, skips, runs, hops, bends, and falls. To these movements, the dancer adds balance, coordination, control, buoyancy, plus a blend of relaxation and tension for continuous motion. The dancer must have a rich vocabulary of movements and know how to give each one a different quality. Through a comprehension of timing, the artist must integrate internal and external rhythms, thus creating melody and harmony. The dancer searches from within for the truest way to express life. This is shared with the audience, and they respond accordingly. Just as music can convey and command emotion without necessarily telling a story, so must dance.

When the art is tap dance, however, one must focus on becoming a percussionist in a more intimate way than other dance forms require. The tap-dancer must sustain a strong rhythmical relationship plus maintain some sort of melody and harmony line. This requires a great deal of concentration and control. The fact that one must be as natural as possible, plus share the joy of the art makes the entire dance seem too complex. Yet the beauty of tap and all dance and art is that it does require a particular commitment in terms of discipline, concentration, and control. It allows us the space for expression and growth, all of which enhance the quality of life.

With the wealth of material that has been covered so far, it would be advantageous to have a thorough review. The usual warm-up exercises (flaps, shuffles, cramprolls, brush-toe-heel in all directions) are performed with each student encouraged to dance alone, doing each step in single, double, and triple time. This is followed with a single, double, and triple time step (Thanks for the Buggy Ride) with emphasis on clarity and accurate timing. A review of the soft shoe and the waltz clog should precede improvisation. As mentioned earlier, experiment with different ways of improvising to eliminate any inhibition on the part of the dancer. Working with your eyes closed or in a darkened room may be helpful, but in any event make the experience of creating and improvising as painless and beneficial as possible because it is here that you can try out new ideas and find new ways to make sound and rhythm. Pullbacks, wings, and barrel turns should also be reviewed with emphasis on staying light and buoyant. At this point, students should be encouraged to create their own routines, either to swing or any suitable contemporary music. Stay simple, use space in large and small ways, and try to overlay rhythms just as you would harmonize with a melody line. Again, simplicity is always preferred because it allows the dancer space for cleanliness and clarity.

In this session the *double shuffle* and a step called the *cross step* will be introduced. These two steps plus three others to be presented in the next chapter compose the Shim Sham, a well-known routine that is a traditional show stopper. The first part of the Shim Sham routine (Figures 7.1–7.13) goes as follows:

Shuffle-step right
Shuffle-step left
Shuffle-step right

Step left

Shuffle-step right

This is repeated on the left and again on the right. The second time you do it on the right it ends differently, like so:

Shuffle-step right
(facing straight ahead, toward audience)

Shuffle-step left

Shuffle-step right

Step left

Shuffle-touch right

Step right

This is followed by a break. Turn 90° to the right.

Touch left

Toe-heel (Step back slightly) left

Toe-heel right

Touch left

Step right (Face forward again)

Step left

Figures 7.1, 7.2, 7.3
Shuffle-step right.

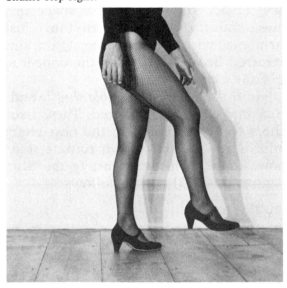

7.1

7.2

7.3
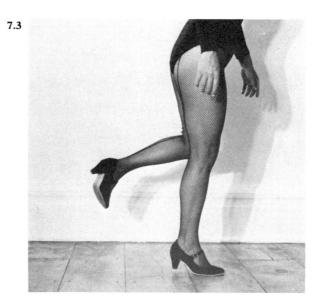

113

Figures 7.4, 7.5, 7.6
Shuffle-step left.

7.4

7.5

7.6

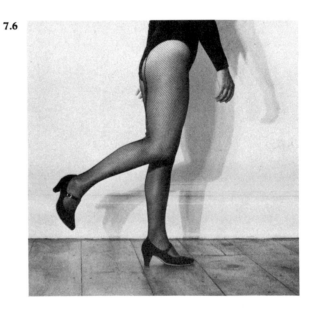

114

Figures 7.7, 7.8, 7.9
Shuffle-step right.

7.7

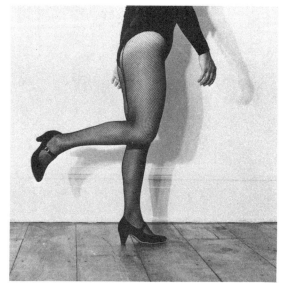

7.8

7.9

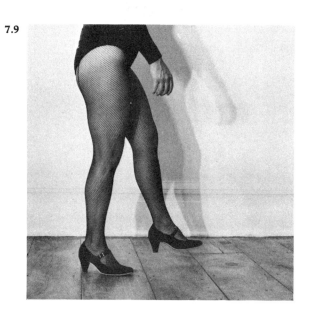

Figure 7.10
Step left.

Figures 7.11, 7.12, 7.13
Shuffle-step.

7.11

7.12

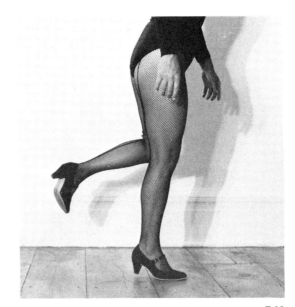

7.13

116

The second step of the Shim Sham (Figures 7.14, 7.15) is a cross step and is danced as follows:

Step right
Touch left
(Bring left foot to meet right
and make a tap sound
by touching ball of left foot to floor)
Step right
Touch left
Toe-heel right
Toe-heel left
Step right

Change directions and repeat to the left and then again to the right, only this time the ending is different.

Figures 7.14, 7.15
Cross step. Step right, touch left, bringing the left foot to meet the right.

7.14

7.15

117

Step right
Touch left
Step right
Touch left
Toe-heel right
Toe-heel left
Step right
Toe-heel left
Toe-heel right
Step left
Toe-heel right
Toe-heel left
Step right
Step left
Step right

JOHN W. BUBBLES

Perhaps one of the most innovative tap masters of his time, John Bubbes started a new style of dancing by adding rythmic complexity to tap. Performing at the age of ten with his six-year-old partner Ford Lee "Buck" Washington, Bubbles danced and acted his way to the top. Perhaps one of the greatest improvisers ever, Bubbles never danced a step the same way twice, and as a result never had his material "borrowed." His unusual accenting and relaxed style led to his success on Broadway, television, and in Hollywood.

LAURENCE "BABY LAURENCE" JACKSON

Baby Laurence was performing at the age of eleven as a singer with the Don Redman Band when he arrived in New York City. His first visit to the Hoofer's Club provided him with a great deal of inspiration, and from then on he became serious about dance. He received some training in dance from Eddie Rector and Harold Mablin, and by the mid-thirties he was working with several acts. He worked with great orchestras such as Count Basie, Woody Herman, and Duke Ellington. His style was initially influenced by Art Tatum and Charlie Parker, and his fundamental interest was in the sounds he could produce, not in movement. An ad lib dancer, Baby Laurence was known to improvise as he went along, staying essentially in one spot, focusing on originality and the complexity of sound.

GENE KELLY

Gene Kelly began his career in vaudeville as a member of the Five Kellys, an act that included all his brothers and sisters. He became well known on Broadway when he starred in *Pal Joey* in 1940, and in Hollywood when he made his screen debut in *For Me And My Gal in 1942*. Kelly worked hard to combine film and dance. His careful organization and arrangement of movement, using all forms of dance and acrobatics, evolved into a unique style. His personality was a significant factor in his films, and he often portrayed a rather brash "All-American" type of guy. Perhaps his most classic film is one that he starred in and codirected, *Singing in the Rain*, a 1952 film about the advent of talkies, which also featured Donald O'Connor and Debbie Reynolds. Kelly's striking cinematic persona gained him the reputation of being one of the most complete film performers ever to come out of Hollywood.

THE NICHOLAS BROTHERS

At the mere ages of eight and fourteen respectively, Harold and Fayard Nicholas opened at the Cotton Club in New York and were an overnight sensation. Together they sang, danced, did acrobatics, and tapped their way into the

119

hearts of all who viewed their performance. Their act was perhaps the best of its time, and it is said that they could imitate anything they saw. George Balanchine had them perform ten-foot leaps that landed in splits for their roles in *Babes in Arms*. Yet their most difficult feat was climbing up a wall of two full steps, then doing backflips, no hands into a split, and bouncing up from the split on the beat! They appeared in several films (where they reportedly appeared at their best) and toured throughout the world, delighting everyone with their charm and talent.

History of Dance

Dance by definition is an art performed by an individual or group where the human body is the instrument, and movement is the medium. The movement is stylized, and the entire dance work is characterized by form and structure. Dance is commonly performed to music or other rhythmic accompaniment. Its primary purpose is the expression of inner feelings and emotions, although it is often performed for social ritual, entertainment, and other purposes.

The earliest record of dance comes from the pre-Christian era. The Chaldeans used dance for educational purposes and are credited with the beginning of astronomy, which they taught by means of great symbolic ballets. Adults would gather in designated areas and configurations and position themselves in accordance with their astrological signs, which conformed with the planets. In reverence to the planets, dances would then be performed as the children watched from the surrounding hills. Dance continued to blossom in ancient Egypt, where it was richly recorded in wall paintings and the literary record of the hieroglyphs. For the Egyptians, who attained an understanding of architectural engineering, astronomy, geometry, and sculpture, dance was the chief medium for religious expression and later evolved into a source of entertainment.

Dance would continue to flourish with an air of magic and mystery. History would tell of dervishes who whirled for twelve to fifteen hours straight without tottering; of

Voodoo dancers from the West Indies who sat practically naked on a metal frame above a fire without being burned; of trance dancers in Indonesia who successively thrust sharp daggers against their bare chests and bent the weapon without inflicting injury on themselves, and of professional dancers in Africa who were necessary to all ceremonies involving the health and well-being of the tribe.

With the discovery of the New World, however, the history of dance endured some interesting twists. Among those who settled in the New World were the Puritans, religious heretics who considered themselves the chosen people. Their doctrine consisted of rigid, hardfast rules, and their principle ethic was "all work and no play." Outside of religion and proper social conditioning for the young, dance was considered "mixt [sic] or promiscuous," and therefore condemned. Although other religious groups, such as the Shakers, incorporated dance as an important part of their ritual, the creed of the Puritans strongly influenced the social acceptance of dance and substantially curtailed its growth in the U.S. New developments would occur in this country upon introduction of African culture, which presented a different style of dancing and singing, plus a new concept of syncopation. From the African and Traditional European modes evolved an entirely new kind of music and dance that would sharply influence future trends.

By the beginning of the twentieth century, a dance craze took place in the U.S. Several new dances emerged from this mania, along with new styles of music. Strongly influenced by different cultures and motivated by a strong need for identity, this new era gave birth to jazz, swing, and ballroom.

Inspired by early minstrels, a style of music known as ragtime evolved. Created by southern blacks, ragtime was set in 2/4 time and featured a persistent syncopation in the melody line. Scott Joplin became one of the most well-known ragtime musicians to popularize this style and set audiences heel tapping to a new kind of rhythm. Concurrently (circa 1912), a musical show called *Over The River* reached New York from San Francisco and featured a dance called the turkey trot. The turkey trot was basically a fast one-step, with the arms pumping at the sides and occassionally flapping in imitation of wild turkeys. The turkey trot was actually contrived by Joseph Smith, son of George Washington Smith, America's first great ballet dancer. This music and new styles of dance set the trends for the dance mania that would sweep America and Europe off their feet.

During this time, a husband and wife dance team emerged who would become the rage of the western world. Irene and Vernon Castle created several new steps which they popularized both in the U.S. and abroad. They were unconventional because they wore contemporary clothing rather than costumes, and as a result they had a great influence on the fashions of the time. Impressed by the Castle image, adults everywhere began to attend dance schools. Another famous couple, Fred Astaire and Ginger Rogers, would later portray the Castles and to some extent continue the style of dancing that so impressed the world in the days prior to World War I.

The following are dances that were popularized in the first half of the twentieth century, many of which are still performed.

Fox Trot The fox trot (Figure 8.1) was introduced in 1914 by a vaude-ville actor named Harry Fox. Fox was performing at the Jardin de Danse on the roof of the New York Theatre, the largest in the world at the time. Part of his act consisted of a certain trotting step that people would start referring to as the fox trot.

Perhaps the most significant development in all of ballroom dancing, the fox trot consisted of a combination of quick and slow steps, offering more variety than other dances of the time and was one of the hardest to learn. A slow variation consisted of forty measures per minute, while the fast version consisted of fifty measures per minute and was named the peabody.

125

Figure 8.1

Charleston In 1924, the Charleston, a zany, feisty, as well as difficult and creative dance, was introduced and soon became the craze in dance halls and on campuses throughout the country (Figure 8.2). Saturday night dance contests were held and the best performer of the Charleston would invariably win. (In Los Angeles, Joan Crawford won every contest.) Historically, the Charleston was derived from a tribal dance originating from the Ibo Tribe in West Africa and was also similar to a well-known dance in Trinidad. Mas-

126

Figure 8.2

tered by many teenagers in the 1920s, the Charleston allowed for the emergence of tap dance and ballroom on a professional level. (Tap-dancers contrived a tap version of the Charleston.) A vernacular dance, the Charleston had a tremendous impact upon the world of dance.

Blackbottom The Blackbottom (Figure 8.3) was made popular by Ann Pennington in George White's *Scandal of 1926*, but had its beginnings much earlier when it was done all over the south. Although its characteristic gesture is the patting of

127

the backside, the dance entails other movements and is best described by its accompanying lyrics:

Hop down front and then you Doodle back
(Doodle is to slide)
Mooch to you left and then you Mooch to the right
Hands on your hips and do the Mess Around
Break-a-leg until you're near the ground
(the Break-a-leg is a limping step)
Now that's the Old Black Bottom Dance

Figure 8.3

Lindy The Lindy was originally performed at the Savoy Ballroom in New York in 1927 (although some say it started earlier), around the time of Lindberg's famous flight to Paris. The Lindy (Figure 8.4) is a syncopated two-step or box step that accents the offbeat, which is followed by a breakaway, the characteristic feature of the step. Although the Lindy received some opposition from the Dance President of the Teachers Business Association who commented that "swing music is a degenerated form of jazz whose devotees are unfortunate victims of economic instability," the Lindy became the craze and swept across the U.S.

Figure 8.4

Known also as the jitterbug, jive, and swing, the Lindy is still a popular social dance.

Rumba The true rumba (Figure 8.5) is of African origin and is indigenously a sexual pantomine danced quickly with exaggerated hip movements. Portraying simple farm tasks such as shoeing a mare or courtship in the barnyard, rumba music is played with a staccato beat in keeping with the powerful movements of the dancers. The American rumba is a modified, slower, and more refined version of the native dance with the same syncopation. Introduced around 1913, the rumba came into vogue in the late twenties with the increased interest in Latin music.

Figure 8.5

Other dances that became popular socially include the samba, a Brazilian step also known as the Carioca Samba (ballroom samba) made famous by Fred Astaire and Ginger Rogers in *Flying Down to Rio,* as well as the merenque, mambo, cha-cha, and the bossa nova.

After the customary warm-up, we will review the exercises learned in the previous chapter, those that comprise the first half of the Shim Sham, and then introduce the second half of the step. The Shim Sham has been a favorite tap routine since the early thirties, and consists of the shuffle-step, the cross step, the Tack Annie (Figures 8.6–8.18), the half-break (Figures 8.19–8.24), and the break step (Figures 8.25–8.28), which occurs three times during the routine. The Shim Sham is the classic finale combination, and the performers often invite dancing members of the audience to join. At one time it became so popular that it evolved into a ballroom step without taps.

The Shim Sham consists of the following:

Shuffle-step:	3 times followed by break
Cross step:	3 times
Tack Annie:	3 times followed by break
Half-break:	2 times followed by break
Half-break:	2 times followed by final step

Tack Annie
Brush-toe step right
(bring right foot behind left)
Brush-toe step left
Brush-toe step right
Brush-toe left
Step right
Step left
(occurs rather fast)

Repeat three times. After the third time, however, you go into the break, so it is danced:

131

Brush-toe step right

Brush-toe step left

Brush-toe step right

Brush-toe left

Step right

Touch-toe-heel left

Toe-heel right

Toe left (body weight on ball of the foot)

Step right

Step left

The following step is called the half-break and is a bouncy sort of step because the body weight continually shifts from side to side. When learning the step, just remember that each body position is a very brief one, so stay nice and light.

Half-Break

Step right

Step left

Shuffle-toe right

Toe left

Repeat the half- break twice and then go into full break. Then repeat half-break twice again, and do the final step that goes as follows:

Final Step

Heel left

Brush-toe right

Heel right

Brush-toe left

Heel left

Brush-toe right

Heel right

Brush-toe left

Figures 8.6, 8.7, 8.8
Brush-toe-step right.

8.6

8.7

8.8

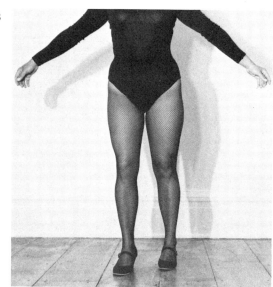

Figures 8.9, 8.10, 8.11
Brush-toe-step left.

8.9

8.10

8.11

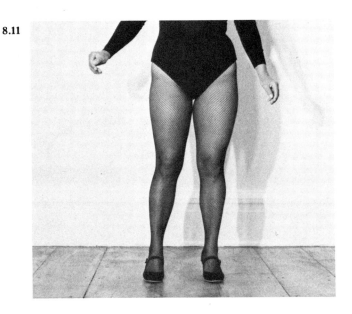

Figures 8.12, 8.13, 8.14
Brush-toe-step right.

8.12

8.13

8.14

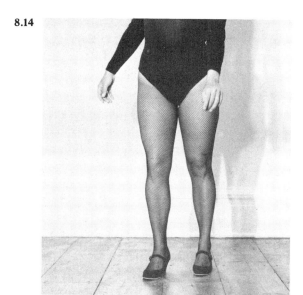

Figures 8.15, 8.16
Brush-toe left.

8.15

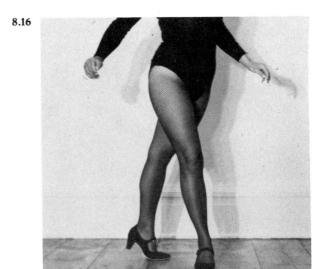

136

Figure 8.17
Step right.

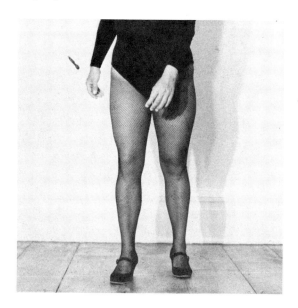

Figure 8.18
Step left.

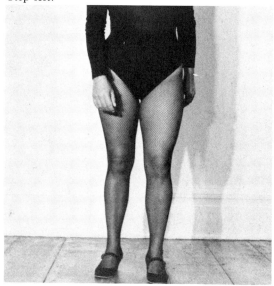

137

Figure 8.19
Step right.

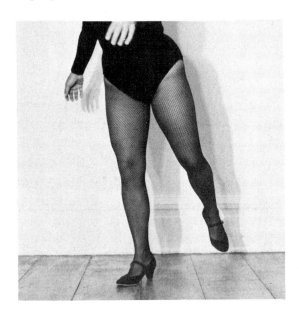

Figure 8.20
Step left.

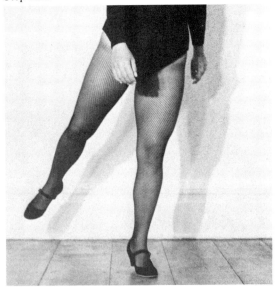

138

Figures 8.21, 8.22, 8.23
Shuffle-step right.

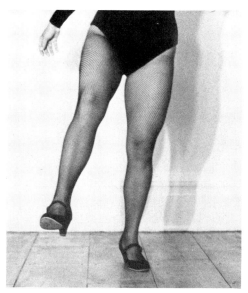

8.21

8.22

8.23

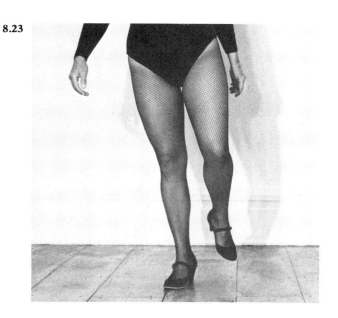

Figure 8.24
Step left.

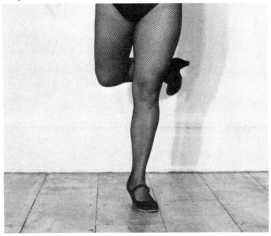

Figures 8.25, 8.26
Heel left.

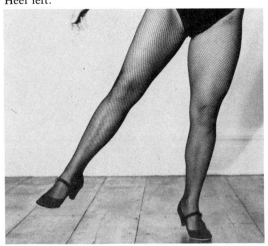

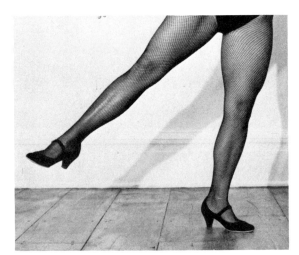

8.25

8.26

Figures 8.27, 8.28
Brush-toe right. Repeat four times alternating sides.

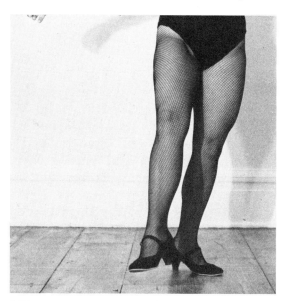

8.27

8.28

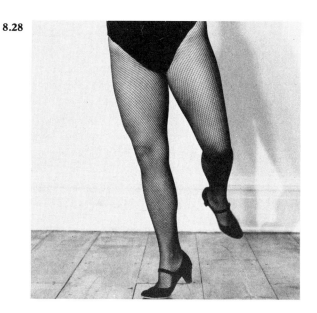

The following are biographical shorts of three of the best female tap-dancers in the twentieth century.

IDA FORSYNE

Born in Chicago in 1883, Ida Forsyne was dancing at the age of ten, working as a pick at the World's Fair. A "pick" was a talented young singer or dancer who was allowed to perform with professional companies. She joined Patti's Black Troubadours at the age of fifteen and worked with the troupe successfully for four years. A tiny woman with a size two shoe, Ida had a blossoming career by 1904, performing Russian and acrobatic dancing. She was described as a "fascinating dancer" and was warmly received throughout Europe for several years. When she returned to the states after nine years abroad, her wonderful career took a turn for the worse, yet she remained true to her art and continued to win the respect of her peers for years to come.

ELEANOR POWELL

Born to dance, Eleanor Powell maintained a reputation of being the most competent female tap-dancer. Her dancing career began very early, and from the start, Eleanor was a stylist and innovative dancer. In her one film with Fred Astaire, *Broadway Melody of 1940*, they did a stunning performance of "Begin The Beguine." Likened to the best male counterparts, Eleanor Powell reputedly had some of the finest feet in the business and, like Astaire and Robinson, she choreographed all of her own material.

ALICE WHITMAN

The youngest of the famed Whitman Sisters, Alice Whitman was one of the best female tap-dancers in show business. Blessed with beauty and talent, Alice was beloved by audiences and fellow dancers alike. She later married Aaron Palmer, also a fine singer and dancer, with whom she had a son named Albert. Albert, nicknamed "Pops," became one of the greatest acrobatic tap-dancers of his time. Known for her good, clean taps, Alice Whitman performed with the Whitman Sisters, and for four decades they remained the royalty of black theater.

History of Tap

Step dancing as it originated in Ireland can be traced back to the fifth century A.D. Within time, the step dances evolved into the Irish Jig, best described by its rapid, complex footwork, accompanied by a rigid upper torso with the arms held fast at the sides. Several centuries later in Lancashire, an industrial English city, another form of foot dancing developed. Similar to the jig in terms of body positioning, the Lancashire Clog was originally performed in wooden clogs. As the dances became more intricate, the clogs became increasingly more hazardous, so they were changed to leather shoes with copper pennies attached to the heels. In another land, thousands of miles away, other forms of dance existed that had an entirely different flavor. In Africa, dances were performed to sophisticated rhythms, and each dancer strove toward individuality. Body movement was emphasized rather than just foot-work. Barefooted dancers would execute a variety of steps with a great deal of skill and agility. In all these countries, dance was an important part of life and health.

What eventually occurred in the New World when the English, Irish, Germans, and Africans arrived was a merger of the various dance forms. What emerged from this blend was a new dance art that would be referred to as America's indigenous dance—tap dance.

Toward the middle of the nineteenth century, a form of entertainment known as minstrelsy became extremely popular in the U.S. and provided a meeting ground for the various cultures and arts that were flocking to this country. Minstrelsy remained a prevalent form of entertainment for well over fifty years, nurturing the growth of song and dance, particularly tap. In minstrelsy, the Afro-American influence became prominent, even though black minstrel companies were not formed until after the Civil War and the emancipation act. But the impact of minstrelsy was profound, and many classic steps were created at this time. The soft shoe evolved from the popular minstrel dance The Essence of Virginia, and it portrayed the more graceful, elegant part of this dance. Another popular dance was the cakewalk. A difficult step that involved a lot of strutting, the cakewalk came into existence on the plantations where blacks imitated the masters. When the masters saw the slaves doing this particular dance, they were so impressed that they decided to hold regular contests, and the winner would receive a piece of cake as a prize! Among the great performers of minstrelsy was a man called William Henry Lane or "Juba," who was the greatest single influence on dance in the nineteenth century. He was known for his well-rounded talent which won him acclaim in the U.S. as well as Europe. George Primrose, another man of Irish heritage, also had a powerful influence on the growth of tap dance in minstrelsy. A wonderful dancer, Primrose furthered the growth of the soft shoe with his finesse and elegance.

Minstrelsy dominated the entertainment world for several years. When its popularity began to wane, it was evident that it lacked versatility and had become stagnant. More importantly, it had eliminated female performers almost entirely and was primarily a masculine form of entertainment. As the demand for something new increased, women became involved in the profession, and a new era was in the making—vaudeville.

Vaudeville gave rise to a new form of family entertainment, which included acrobatics, singing, dancing, and comedy and remained influential for many decades. An unfortunate aspect of vaudeville was that it remained segregated and resulted in white and black vaudeville coexisting separately. Black vaudeville was T.O.B.A. (Theatre Owners Booking Association) and was founded by Sherman Dudley prior to World War I. T.O.B.A. booked acts in the North and South, giving rise to several talented performers. Among the acts of this time were the Berry Brothers, a well-known acrobatic team; Eddie Rector, who gave elegance and full body movement to the form; the Whitman Sisters, the most prestigious company of its time; King Rastus Brown, a noted buck dancer who radically changed the art of tap, and Bill Robinson, who brought tap dancing up on the toes (where the dance is done primarily on the balls of the feet). White vaudevillians included James Barton, a very influential dancer who employed comedy and legomania to his dance;

George M. Cohan, a multifaceted performer who started his career in vaudeville; the Condos Brothers, originators of the Five Tap Wing; Harland Dixon, skilled in pantomime, and Pat Rooney, known for his wonderful version of the waltz clog.

Between 1909 and 1920, something called "dance madness" prevailed in the U.S. and gave rise to several new dances such as the fox trot, the turkey trot, the grizzly bear, and the bunny hug. This paved the way for Irene and Vernon Castle, who made a very large impact on social dancing, both in this country and abroad. Trends established in social dancing during this period changed conventional styles that had reigned up until the turn of the century. Couple dancing was no longer dictated by fixed rules. Adults studied ballroom, and everybody danced.

Prior to World War I, tap dancing incorporated different styles to increase its scope and appeal. American tap-dancers adapted Russian dancing to their style, giving tap a vigorous new dimension that included splits, turns, spins, and jumps. Accomplished in this style were Ida Forsyne and Dewey Weinglass. Another form blended with tap was acrobatics, which added lots of flash to the art. Masters of acrobatic tap included Archie Ware, Willie Covan, and Maxie McCree. Exceptional acrobatic acts included The Four Covans, Tip, Tap & Toe, and the Four Step Brothers. In later years, Albert "Pops" Whitman would become one of the greatest acrobatic tap-dancers to ever hit the stage.

In the early twenties a show called *Shuffle Along* opened on Broadway and proceeded to revolutionize the stage. It was the most popular black musical to ever play in all theaters from coast to coast, and it introduced the "chorus line," sixteen females dancing in unison. The musical set a new precedence for dance, music, and theater along with creating such stars as Eubie Blake and Bill "Bojangles" Robinson.

The first black dancing star on Broadway, Bill Robinson, began dancing in the late eighteen hundreds, but it was not until he was fifty years old that he won the attention of the media through his performance in *Black-*

150

birds of 1928. This feisty, talented man brought tap dancing up on the toes and provided inspiration for many of the dancers who were coming up at the time, such as Bill Bailey. Also prominent during this time was John Bubbles, an innovative dancer who created a new style of dancing. Bubbles' craft and ingenuity added rhythmic complexity to tap, which he accomplished by including the use of the heels. A well-rounded performer, Bubbles danced, sang, and acted successfully throughout his lucrative career. In Hollywood, Fred Astaire began his career in musical films, where he would achieve extraordinary eclat, dancing his way into the hearts of millions.

As tap composition increased in complexity during the twenties and thirties, tap dancing continued to develop as an art form. More body movement was used to accommodate the steps, flash steps became more arduous, and the blend of the various cultures combined more thoroughly. Classic routines were designed at this time that added flash, movement, and more interesting rhythmic concepts. From this evolved two new acts: flash and class. Flash acts sparkled with rapid, precise steps that were extravagant as well as difficult. The Berry Brothers and the Nicholas Brothers were among the most famous. The other kind of act was a class act. These acts often consisted of two or three people who performed a variety of routines which included a soft shoe performed at a painstakingly slow tempo and executed with enormous ease and elegance. Pioneers of the class act were Eddie Rector, Aaron Palmer, and Maxie McCree, as well as Greenlee and Drayton, The Three Dukes, The Lucky Seven Trio, and Pete, Peaches, and Duke. The last great class act was Coles and Atkins, who were known for their marvelous skills in tap dancing. They played with all the great swing bands throughout the U.S. and Europe and choreographed all their own material for *Gentlemen Prefer Blondes*, which they performed for two years on Broadway.

In the fifties, new trends were occurring in theater. Tastes were changing, and the demand for something new and different prevailed. In the process, the desire for tap temporarily diminished, and the call for tap dancing in

151

George Tapps and his dancers, A Nightclub Tap Unit. Photo by Zachary Freyman.

productions decreased substantially. Many professionals felt that tap died at this time. Others decided to remain with the form and somehow managed to keep it going. Up until this point, the history of tap dance had gone virtually unrecorded.

Owing to the avid interest of people such as Marshall and Jean Stearns who spent years collecting all the data that comprise their anthology *Jazz Dance* (MacMillan, 1968), Leticia Jay who coordinated the *Tap Happening* in New York City (1969), which assimilated several of the tap meisters for the first time in years and others such as Brenda Bufalino, who began to document the history of the art and produced *Great Feats of Feet,* tap managed to undergo a resurgence in the seventies.

The demand for tap began to increase at a soaring pace. Many Broadway shows included tap, the media began paying more attention to the form, and several revivals began highlighting it. Tap classes filled up all over the country. As though nothing had ever happened, tap dance won the admiration of audiences all over the world.

10
The Future

The resurgence of tap created an arena for the continuance of the form. As a result, a new group of devotees emerged who were equipped with the enthusiasm necessary for working in the art. Some had been involved in tap for many years and would pass on the art, creating new concepts of rhythm and movement. Others who had been reared in the medium and had danced most of their lives had not yet made a definitive statement. There were also those who were just discovering that tap indeed existed and were suddenly swept away in a new pursuit. Different talents would emanate to cultivate the art and its appeal. Broadway and Hollywood would become home for people like Gregory Hines, a wonderful performer and tap-dancer. Motivated by a love for the form, a whole new generation would mature with many different concepts.

The following conversations are with a few artists who have grown with the form in recent years.

GAIL CONRAD

"Tap is a very rich art form and when I conceptualize about it, I think of melody, rhythm, and conversation," says Gail Conrad. A gifted performer and choreographer, Gail started dancing as a child. She was in and out of touch with dance throughout adolescence, but returned to modern and tap and began using both mediums to express her image of dance. She studied with Charles Cooke (from Cooke and Brown), and later became a tap teacher in downtown Manhatten where she experimented with some of her concepts on theater groups. By 1978, she had formed a company of dancers who were well skilled in all forms of dance. Although the members have changed, the company continues to perform quite successfully in the New York area.

"I find the visual part of tap to be very important because it creates its own atmosphere." As a result, Gail's choreography is alive with imagery and dreamlike qualities. "The dances are like small stories or vignettes." She envisions her choreography in film concepts and makes a picture through the dance. When it comes to teaching tap material, Gail enjoys observing how people incorporate movement, get the feeling of dancing, and utilize the entire body.

In terms of keeping an art (particularly tap) alive, Gail feels the most important thing is to rejuvenate on an artistic and personal level. "You can't just do revivalist work. It is important to be aware of history and remain creative."

Gail Conrad Tap Dance Theatre.
Photo by John Elbers.

PAT GIORDANO

A lithe, sensitive dancer, Pat Giordano began studying at the age of three and can remember that she wanted to go to dancing school more than anything else in the world. For several years, she trained in all forms of dance, but tap was always her favorite. During the time that she stopped tap dancing, she would always keep a pair of tap shoes in her closet to amaze her friends.

Pat finds the nostalgic element of tap to be somewhat frightening. "There are so few dancers that can really do it (tap), that they must all take the responsibility to keep it alive and bring it further along. It must evolve." She finds that teaching is an opportunity to pass on information in a historical sense, but that her function is not to simply repeat what she has learned. "It is important for me to develop something new. I experiment while I am teaching and I balance it with the needs of the students."

"People think tap is easy because in the theater they have seen little kids do it (the Shirley Temple image), or people who can really tap but are forced to play subservient roles. All of this had done little to show the virtuosity of the form." As a result, she feels that people carry around the image that tap is simple and that anyone can do it. "Tap takes years. It can take forever to perfect a routine because there is always room to find new subtleties, new accents or new ways of presenting the same material. The subtleties of tap make an enormous difference."

"I have been intrigued with tap all my life. The process of struggling and breaking through excites me. It gives me a real opportunity to watch myself."

JANE GOLDBERG

When Jane Goldberg came to New York to study tap, she studied with several great hoofers, but Charles Cooke became her real inspiration. Jane studied with Cooke and later organized shows that featured them both doing tap, comedy, and song.

Jane began to gather information on tap's past and learning the history became her task. In 1979, she founded the Changing Times Tap Company, which was designed to preserve, promote, and perform tap dance. Two years later she organized By Word of Foot, a tap dance festival that reunited several great tap artists who performed, lectured, and demonstrated their skills to an audience of tap enthusiasts from all over the country. This festival was an effort to show that rhythms could be broken down and learned. It was a wonderful success, a warm, inspiring experience for all those who participated.

"Fun involves teaching the tradition, telling people the origin of the steps and who did them. I love teaching history with the steps. Sometimes it is easy to forget what an amazing art tap dance is, but teaching keeps you in touch with your love for the form."

This is only a small picture of what is happening in the world of tap today. It portrays a particular kind of artist with a strong sentiment for creativity and history. If the art is to continue and evolve, it will take people such as these to enhance the form.

Dance   1/10   Anna Marie Ottaviano 82

"Dance" by Anna Marie Ottaviano

163